Twelve Becoming

Biographies of Mennonite Disciples from the Sixteenth to the Twentieth Century

TWELVE BECOMING

Biographies of Mennonite Disciples from the Sixteenth to the Twentieth Century

Cornelius J. Dyck   Illustrated by Richard Loehle

FAITH AND LIFE PRESS
NEWTON, KANSAS

International Standard Book Number 0-87303-865-7

Library of Congress Number 73-75174

Printed in the United States of America
Copyright © 1973 by Faith and Life Press
724 Main Street, Newton, Kansas 67114

For the story of Christopher Dock the author
acknowledges primary dependence on *Christopher
Dock, Colonial Schoolmaster*, by Gerald C. Studer.
© 1967 by Herald Press, Scottdale, Pa.

The poem "Brown Peace Pipes" by Alexander
Posey is reprinted from the book *Broken Peace
Pipes* with the permission of the author, Irvin M.
Peithmann.

Except where otherwise indicated, the Bible
quotations in this volume are in accordance with
the Revised Standard Version of the Bible,
copyright © 1946 and 1971, by the Division of
Christian Education of the National Council of
Churches of Christ in the United States of
America, and are used by permission.

Other versions of the Bible quoted in this book
are as follows:
On pages 51 and 59, *Today's English Version
of the New Testament*. Copyright © American
Bible Society, 1966, 1971. Used by permission.

On pages 89, 95, and 97, *The Living Bible
Paraphrased*. Copyright © 1971, Tyndale House
Publishers. Used by permission.

On pages 119 and 126, *The New English Bible,*
Copyright © The Delegates of the Oxford
University Press and The Syndics of the Cambridge
University Press, 1961, 1970. Reprinted by
permission.

Designed by John Hiebert
Printed by Mennonite Press, Inc.

To Wilma and our daughters
Mary, Jenny, and Sue

Preface

Twelve Becoming is for you. The author has written a book that is readable for a wide age range. Whether you are a boy or girl, a grandmother or grandfather, I think you will enjoy reading it.

Twelve Becoming is an unusual title, isn't it? Everything that is alive is becoming something. A seed becomes a seedling, tender and green. Then it becomes a sturdy plant. More changes occur and it becomes a flower. Still more changes and seeds appear. The plant becomes old and finally dies. Only then does it stop becoming.

The twelve stories in this book are about people trying to become what God wanted them to be. All these people had or have a part in the history of our church. I hope that as you read these stories and learn about these people, they will help you in becoming what God wants you to be. This is why the Commission on Education asked Cornelius J. Dyck to write these stories.

Twelve Becoming can be used in a variety of ways. You can read it by yourself. It can also be used in family settings such as at mealtime or during family devotions. It can also be used in small study groups such as Sunday school classes.

The Commission on Education wishes to thank the author for the work he has done in helping *Twelve Becoming* to become a book. Since he too has a family, he has been able to make this book one that will be especially useful in this setting. He is also professor of historical theology at the Associated Mennonite Biblical Seminaries which adds to his qualifications as the author of this book.

> Frank G. Ward
> Commission on Education
> General Conference Mennonite Church

Acknowledgements

The author gratefully acknowledges the help of the following persons with the stories as specified:

"Christopher Dock": Gerald C. Studer.

"John H. Oberholtzer": J. Herbert Fretz and Albert E. Hornberger.

"David Toews": His daughter Louise (Toews) Friesen and her husband Blake.

"Cornelius F. Klassen": His sister Elfrieda (Klassen) Dyck and her husband Peter, his son Herbert Klassen, and former secretary Doreen Harms.

"Nicolai Siemens": His daughter Frieda (Siemens) Kaethler and her husband Willie.

"Harold S. Bender": His wife Elizabeth (Horsch) Bender, daughter Mary Eleanor, sister Florence, and former colleagues Melvin Gingerich and Nelson P. Springer.

"Ngongo David": Ngongo David, George Neufeld, James Bertsche, and the staff of Africa Inter-Mennonite Mission.

"Lena Graber": Lena Graber and her sister Esther.

"Joe Walks Along": Joe Walks Along, Malcolm Wenger, and David Habegger.

"Suhadiweko Djojodihardjo": Suhadiweko Djojodihardjo, Wilbert Shenk, and Mesach Krisetya.

Particular appreciation for their patience and encouragement is also expressed to Harold Buller, Willard Claassen, Orlando Waltner, Frank G. Ward, and James Dunn, present or past members of the Commission on Education of the General Conference Mennonite Church.

The author is, nevertheless, finally responsible for the material presented here.

C.J.D.

Contents

MENNO SIMONS   13
1496-1561

CHRISTOPHER DOCK   21
    -1771

JOHANN CORNIES   29
1789-1848

JOHN H. OBERHOLTZER   39
1809-1895

DAVID TOEWS   51
1870-1947

CORNELIUS (C. F.) KLASSEN   61
1894-1954

NICOLAI SIEMENS   69
1895-1958

HAROLD S. BENDER   79
1897-1962

NGONGO DAVID   89

LENA GRABER   97

JOE WALKS ALONG   111

SUHADIWEKO DJOJODIHARDJO   119

Menno Simons
1496-1561

Menno threw his cards on the table and got up. "I'm tired of playing cards all day," he said angrily to the two priests with him. "This is no life for a priest of the church! Surely God has more important things for us to do than eat and drink, say a mass a day, or two, and grow fat."

"There he goes again," one of the two muttered to the other, and then he added more loudly, "Menno, why are you so moody lately, always grumbling and asking questions about the Bible and the church? Why can't you just be a good priest and mind your own business like we've told you a hundred times? Who do you think you are, the Pope?" With that they got up and left the room.

Alone in the room, Menno walked to the window and gazed out into the grey dusk of evening. It was winter. Heavy fog was rolling in over the dikes from the North Sea barely ten miles away. How he loved his native Holland, and especially the little town of Witmarsum in the northern tip of the land! He had been born here. Most of his aunts and uncles and cousins lived nearby. He remembered how he used to play with his cousins on the dikes and swim together with them in the canals. He remembered his father's farm with the windmill, and the house and barn all under one roof. He wished he were a boy again. And then he heard the little bell. It was time to eat.

That night he could not sleep. Even after he blew out the short tallow candle he kept thinking and thinking. He thought of the time when his father Simon had called him to his big chair and said, "Menno, your mother and I want you to become a priest in the church. It is a great privilege to serve God and man as a priest. God will bless you. Do you think you are ready for it?"

"If you say so, Father," he had replied, for he had been only nine years old. "What if I don't like it? Will I always have to be a priest for the rest of my life anyway?"

"You will like it," his father had replied. "God will help you."

"And what must I do now?" he had asked.

"I will talk to the priest about it next week. I think you have to go to the St. Francis school in the monastery."

And so it had turned out. As he lay there thinking, it seemed as though it had happened only yesterday. But most of all he thought about all the new things he had been reading in the Bible. He had never really read the Bible until now, even as a priest. It was all so new and strange. The roosters were beginning to crow in the village barns when he finally fell asleep.

The new day brought more things for Menno to think about. While walking across the yard to the church he met one of the other priests who asked, "Have you heard what happened in Leeuwarden yesterday?"

"No," he replied, "what happened?"

"A man named Sicke Snyder was executed for having himself baptized a second time," he answered. "They chopped off his head. Serves him right. He was a heretic."

"Strange!" thought Menno, "why would an adult have himself baptized if he had already been baptized as a child? And why would the authorities execute him just for that? Does the government have a right to tell people what to believe?" As soon as he was finished in church he went to his room again to see if the Bible might have an answer to his question.

DISCOVERING THE BIBLE

In those days all people were baptized as little children. It was believed that they would go to hell if they were not. Menno had baptized many children himself. Now he wanted to find the places in the Bible where it spoke of baptism, especially the baptism of children.

The Bible Menno used was written in the Latin language, but he had fortunately learned to read the Latin. He read for days and weeks whenever he had time. He read chapter after chapter, but he could not find what he was looking for. "Isn't it strange," he said to himself one day. "Here I have been baptizing all these children and I can't find a place in the Bible where it says they are lost unless I do so." And then he found the place in Matthew 19:14 where Jesus had told His disciples, "Let the children come to me, and do not hinder them; for to such belongs the kingdom of heaven."

Gradually it became clear to Menno that heaven is the gift of God to those who believe in Jesus and obey Him, whether they are baptized or not. One

day while he was eating dinner with the two priests who worked with him he said, "I've been reading the Bible a lot lately."

"Yes, we know," one of them answered. Then the other added, "That's dangerous."

Menno continued, "The Bible doesn't seem to say that we should baptize children. God loves them and will take care of them. Baptism is for adults who have heard the gospel, believe it, and are ready to live by it. Children can't understand a sermon when they are eight days old, nor can they believe it, or make any decisions about how they are going to live."

The two men shook their heads. "You are wrong, Menno," one of them said. "The church teaches that we should baptize infants. The church is always right. Remember what happened to Sicke Snyder."

"Yes," the other added, "remember Snyder."

But Menno knew that he was right because the Bible just seemed to prove itself true as he read it. Studying it was like sailing over the ocean and discovering a whole new continent, or finding a new planet in the sky. He had never heard anyone speak of the meaning of faith the way the Bible did. He came to believe that the Bible should be the final authority about what he should believe and do, and that what other men or the church said would have to agree with it if he was to believe them.

HIDING TO SAVE HIS LIFE

For a time Menno stayed in the church at Witmarsum. Yet his Bible studies and prayers had worked a great change in him, a conversion to follow Christ completely. Gradually he found courage to talk about his new faith in Christ to others, even in his sermons. People found this helpful. They often walked many miles to hear him. Soon he was known as the "great evangelical preacher of Witmarsum."

But some people hated him. He was trying to change them, and they did not want to be changed. The two priests working with him became increasingly suspicious of what he was doing. He knew they were reporting everything to the bishop. "Menno," they would argue, "you are trying to change the church. But the church has not changed for a thousand years. It is the ark which saves all who are in it, like Noah was saved in the flood."

Menno would reply, "No, the church is not an ark; it cannot save anyone. It is to be a light to show people to Jesus, like a lighthouse guides ships in a harbor at night." But he knew his time was up. He would have to flee soon if he wished to escape imprisonment and possibly even death. He knew that the church often asked the government to arrest and execute people who disagreed with it.

Early one morning, while the village was still sleeping, he stole out of the house and began walking to the city of Groningen. Because there would be many people in the city he hoped to go unnoticed among them. Instead of the long black robe of a priest he wore the clothing of an ordinary worker. On his back he carried a sack which now contained everything he owned, including a Bible and some books by Martin Luther. He walked all day, and when night came, a haystack in the field became his bed. He was tired and lonely, but he was also happy, for he knew he was doing the will of God.

Late next day he came to the city and knocked on the door of a friend's house. For a moment the friend did not recognize Menno in his strange clothing. "Why

it's you!" he finally said. "What is going on? Are you in trouble? Come in, come in." He knew about Menno's new faith and agreed with it. There were many in Groningen who believed the same way. "Tell me what happened," he urged Menno. "I have often wondered how long you would be safe in Witmarsum. You have been speaking up so boldly lately."

They talked long into the night. "It is clear that you must stay in hiding," his friend said. "We have a room in which you are safe. But you must not leave the house."

Menno stayed in that house for nine months without his enemies finding him. Sometimes when it was very dark he would go outside to see the stars and breathe fresh air, but he spent most of his time reading the Bible and writing. He called one of his first writings *The New Birth* because it described how he had been changed when he came to know and love Jesus. In it he said: "In your life you must be so converted and changed that you become new men in Christ, so that Christ is in you and you are in Christ. Otherwise you can never be Christians, for, 'if any one is in Christ, he is a new creation' (2 Cor. 5:17)."

One evening they heard voices outside the house. Soon there was a knock at the door. Menno looked at his friend and said, "I think they have found me at last. God's will be done."

But his friend answered, "I don't know who it is. Go to your room. I will answer the door."

Six men came in, but they were not Menno's enemies. They were friends.

"Brother Menno," one of them began, "we have been looking for you. We are of one heart and mind with you. We believe in Jesus, too."

"Yes," another of them said, "and

there are many hundreds, perhaps thousands, in the land who are with us in the faith."

"But," they continued, "we all need help. We need someone to lead us and unite us. Wherever we go we hear about your good work in Witmarsum. We believe God is calling you to be our leader, and have come to ask you to accept."

Menno was quiet for a long time. "I am not a leader," he finally said. "I just want to serve and follow Jesus. You are right. The old church will not change. It is not the true church. The true church is made up of all who believe in Jesus as their Savior as the Bible teaches and who are ready to follow Him as Lord of everything they do. I know there are many who believe this. They often came to the services in Witmarsum. I could tell by the way they looked at me and talked to me that they were different."

"We used to come to Witmarsum, too," one of the men interrupted Menno. "We heard you preach and teach. That is why we are here to call you."

"But," Menno went on, "do you know what you are asking me to do? I am afraid to say yes to your request. Don't you know that church and government will do everything they can to catch me? If they do, they will torture me and then burn me alive. I don't want to be burned alive. I want to be alive and free."

It was very quiet in the room after he said that. What he had said was true. He would be hunted like a criminal. A reward would be offered for his arrest or information leading to his arrest. He would be called a heretic. Heretics were often believed to have sold themselves to the devil. People thought they were dangerous and should be killed because they led others from the "true" faith.

Then Menno himself broke the silence. "But I did not promise to follow Jesus

only if it were easy. My life is in His hands, no matter what the cost. If He wants me to do this thing, I will, gladly. But is it really His will? Give me time to think it over. I will send word to you soon."

Then, after they had prayed together for wisdom and courage, the men went home.

Not long after this visit another man came to see Menno, a minister named Obbe Philips. After they had talked about their faith and about the call Menno had received, Menno said, "Obbe, will you baptize me?"

That evening, in the presence of a few friends who had been invited, Menno told of his faith experiences and his decision to leave the old church. Obbe asked him, "Do you believe in Jesus Christ as your Lord and Savior?"

Menno replied, "I do, with all my heart."

"Do you," Obbe continued, "promise to serve him faithfully all the days of your life, no matter what may come?"

Menno replied again, "I do, with all my heart."

Then as he knelt, Obbe baptized him with water, saying, "I baptize you in the name of the Father, and of the Son, and of the Holy Spirit. Amen."

Before the visitors left, Menno said, "Tell the men who came to see me that I accept their call as a call from God. I am leaving tomorrow to begin my work."

GERTRUDE

So Menno was on the move once again. He wanted to go wherever faithful men and women were ready to hear the gospel, to study the Bible together, and to win others. But travel was difficult and dangerous in the sixteenth century.

Most people walked, though tickets could be bought for stagecoaches and canal and riverboats. Menno usually walked. There is a story about Menno's travel which may be a legend. One day, the story goes, as he was riding on the outside front seat of a coach together with the driver because the seats inside were taken, a group of soldiers rode up and stopped the coach. "Is Menno Simons in there?" they asked the men on the driver's seat.

Menno climbed down, opened the door of the coach, and called in, "Is Menno Simons in there?" The people inside answered, "No."

Whereupon he turned to the soldiers and said, "They say he is not in there," and the soldiers rode away.

It was on one of these trips that Menno Simons met Gertrude. She was a charming young woman, he thought, and he liked her cooking. Most of all he liked her faith in God. Wouldn't it be wonderful, he said to himself, to have a home to go to and a wife to talk with about all his joys and problems. But then he remembered that he was being hunted by his enemies, and that he would probably never have a home of his own. They might catch him tomorrow and kill him. So he left to continue his journey. But he came back again and again. And one day he asked her to marry him. "I have no home," he told her, "no salary, no furniture. I have only my faith in God and my love for you."

"Menno," she replied, "to serve God faithfully is more important to me than a home or money."

Soon they were married. They had no honeymoon. They hid in the barns and basements and attics of friends instead. But they knew they were doing God's will, and that He would take care of them.

It was indeed fortunate that they loved each other, for poor Gertrude had a difficult time of it. How could she cook without a kitchen, and how could she plant a garden when they were always moving in order not to be found out? Besides, Menno was gone most of the time.

One day when he came home from a long journey Gertrude met him at the door and said, "I have a surprise for you." And there in a little cradle lay their baby boy. "He looks just like you," she added.

"What shall we name him?" Menno asked.

"I think we should call him Jan," she replied.

And Jan it was. Later Jan had two sisters, but we do not know their names. They were often sick. Once when Gertrude called a doctor he said, "Mrs. Simons, what these children need is better food and more sunshine. Get them out of this wet basement immediately."

But how could she when she had no home of her own and no other place to go? Jan died a few years later from all the hardships.

How thankful Gertrude felt whenever Menno came home safely from his travels! Then he would play with the children and tell them stories about his adventures until they fell asleep. And late into the night he would talk with her about what God was doing among the people, how more and more were finding joy and peace by trusting Jesus. But he also told of many who were drowned and burned because of their faith. Sometimes he would disguise himself and would stand in the crowd watching the execution of one of his Christian friends. He would feel like shouting for help, but knew that it would do no good; they would only get him, too. So instead, he would give some secret sign to the dying martyr to let him know he was there praying for him.

One day he came home deeply troubled. "Gertrude," he said, "two of my best friends in Witmarsum, Herman and Gerrit Jans, were executed because they took me in for the night. They were reported by their neighbors. Is it right to visit anyone anymore if they are going to suffer so because of it?"

"But they want you to come," she replied. "They want your help in Bible study and they want you to baptize new believers."

A SAFE PLACE TO LIVE

One day soon after Christmas in 1542 a friend came to Menno and showed him a clipping from a paper. It was a decree issued against Menno and his followers by the Emperor Charles V: "A reward of one hundred dutch guilders in gold is hereby offered by his Majesty Emperor Charles V for any information leading to the arrest of one Menno Simons, leader of the Anabaptists . . . dead or alive . . . . Anyone caught giving him food or shelter or help in any way will be executed. . . ."

"Gertrude," Menno said, "it is time for us to leave again. Do you know that they executed Claes Jansz Brongers in Leeuwarden because he took me in for the night the last time I preached there? We must move on."

This time they crossed the border into Germany. There Countess Anna ruled the province of East Friesland. Some of Menno's friends were already living there and she liked them. They were peaceful and hard-working citizens. She too had issued a decree, but instead of trying to kill Menno, she said that all who were as good as he was, all *Menists,* as she called them, were welcome in her land. By

Menists she meant the followers of Menno. Soon everybody was calling them by that name, or *Menonists*. They did not mind, though they would rather people simply called them *Christians*—after Christ.

At last Menno was free to write and work in peace. He even had a home on the large estate of a nobleman. "Gertrude," he said, "now you can plant your garden. And you even have a kitchen. We have never had it so good."

Several days later a wagon loaded with big machine parts drove up to the house. "Menno," Gertrude asked, "what is that?"

"That, my dear," he replied with enthusiasm, "is a printing press. I have long hoped and prayed for a small press to print literature for the groups of believers. In that way I can reach every one of them."

"And where," she asked with a sinking feeling, "are you going to put that big thing?"

"Why," he replied, "I thought we could put it into our big room." And they did. Gertrude did her best to get along with the mess and the clatter it made all day and into the night.

One of the most important books Menno wrote and printed there was *The Foundation Book*. He gave it that title because of the Bible verse, 1 Corinthians 13:11, which meant more to him than any other and which he quoted as follows: "There can be no other foundation beyond that which is already laid; I mean Jesus Christ himself." The book described what the Mennonites believed. True Christians, he wrote, are baptized only after they have experienced a new birth. They love all men, even their enemies. They are willing to suffer and die for their faith. They are eager to tell others about it. They always speak the truth. They know that God rules the world and

they need not fear the future. They gather often to help each other, to study the Bible, and to celebrate the Lord's Supper. And, he wrote, they can do this only when Jesus Christ is the center of their life.

GROWING OLD

An opportunity soon came for Menno and his people to show that they really loved others. Menno was visiting the congregation in Wismar, a city on the northern coast of Germany, when several boys came running into the house. "Mr. Simons," they reported, "a big ship is stuck in the ice in the harbor. It is full of people, too."

Menno went out to investigate and found that they were refugees from England. They were indeed stuck and needed help. He went to the mayor of the city, but the mayor told Menno, "We will not help them. They believe differently than we do. They can help themselves." So Menno and his followers immediately gathered food and clothing and money and took it to the ship. When the people were able to leave the ship the Mennonites invited them into their humble homes until they could travel on. Some were grateful for the help, but some refused to come. "You believe differently than we do," they said. "We don't need your help."

By this time Menno was beginning to grow old. Church leaders came from far away to see him and talk over their problems with him. Menno had seen much suffering and had suffered much himself. His spiritual roots had gone deep down into the strong grace of God, and so he was able to help and comfort many others.

Sometimes, however, he felt discouraged. The people in the church did not love each other enough. They were still scattered and often divided. Persecution had made them afraid to witness to others about their faith. They were content to be left alone to work hard and be good farmers. Gertrude had died soon after they came to Germany, and so he was often alone. On one of his trips to Wismar he had injured his knee and from then on had to use a cane to walk. Perhaps it was the very trip in which he helped the refugees—we do not know. After that he often signed his letters simply, "Your brother, the cripple."

Yet deep down Menno Simons was truly happy. God had been very good to him and to the church. Thousands had come to know Jesus because of the work he had done. The blessing of God had made him very rich in heart and spirit, though he was poor in money and other possessions.

Instead of being executed for his faith as he often thought he would be, Menno died peacefully in his own home at the age of sixty-five. It was on Friday, January 31, 1561, twenty-five years and one day after he left the old church in Witmarsum. He was buried in the garden behind his house.

Many years later a beautiful obelisk was erected to mark the place where he was buried. When it became old and needed to be replaced, a new marker was erected by the students of the University of Kiel in 1953. They did it to show their gratitude to the Mennonites for helping them with food and clothing immediately following the war, just as Menno would have done long ago.

1

Christopher Dock
-1771

? 1693
7 8

Love never ends. 1 CORINTHIANS 13:8

"Dear child, as soon as you are called in the morning, arise; indeed, accustom yourself to 'awaken' at the proper time without being called, and to rise without loitering.

"When you have left your bed, turn back the covers.

"Let your first thoughts be turned toward God, after the example of David, who (Psalm 139:18) saith: 'When I awake, I am still with Thee.'

"Bid a good morning to those whom you meet first and to your parents, sisters and brothers; not from mere habit, but do it out of true love.

"Accustom yourself to dress quickly, but at the same time neatly.

"Instead of idle talk with your sisters and brothers, seek while dressing to have good thoughts . . . .

"When you wash your face and hands, do not splash water about the room.

"Rinsing the mouth with water each morning and rubbing the teeth with the fingers serves to preserve the teeth.

"In combing your hair do not stand in the middle of the room, but in a corner.

"Your morning prayer should be said, not as a matter of indifferent habit, but in fervent gratitude to God who has guarded you during the night; pray Him humbly to bless your actions this day; neither forget to sing, and to read the Bible.

"Do not eat your breakfast on the street or in school, but ask your parents to give it to you at home.

"Then gather up your books and come to school in proper time."

These "Rules for the conduct of a child in the house of its Parents" were written over two hundred years ago in colonial Pennsylvania. Do they sound strange to you? How do they make you feel? The man who wrote them was Christopher Dock, a schoolteacher whom almost everybody loved. Perhaps we can understand his rules better if we get to know him and the time in which he lived.

DOCK COMES TO SKIPPACK

Christopher Dock came to Pennsylvania in 1718. An old document gives the following account of his coming: "Dock came from Germany where he had been drafted in the army. Having conscientious scruples against fighting, he asked for his release, and upon being refused, he made a vow that if God would help him escape he would go to America and devote his remaining days to the education of the youth in the new land. He fortunately was able to make his escape. . . ."

We know very little about his early life. He taught school in Germany for four years before he came to America. This means he may have been as old as twenty-five when he arrived, or even a little older. The ocean voyage must have been quite an ordeal, since it often lasted

1718
1693

twelve weeks or longer. Food was usually scarce and often poor. Many people would be ill or seasick. Sometimes they died on the way and were buried at sea. But Dock left no record of his travel experiences. We can only imagine what might have happened.

Pennsylvania was a Quaker colony when Dock arrived. The Quakers were friends of the Mennonites. King Charles II of England had given the whole state of Pennsylvania to the Quaker William Penn in 1681. This was to pay a debt which the king owed William's father. Penn immediately invited settlers from Germany, France, Holland, and England to make his new land their home, and many, including Mennonites, came.

When the first Mennonites came to Pennsylvania in 1683, they settled six miles north of Philadelphia, which had just been established. They called their new settlement Germantown. A congregation was soon organized and in 1708 the first meetinghouse was built. This was the first Mennonite church in America. During the week it was used as a school.

Meanwhile other German settlers, including Mennonites, were arriving, but instead of staying in the Germantown area they went twenty or more miles farther northwest to Skippack Creek, where they began to farm. In 1717, one year before Dock arrived, a Dutch Mennonite named Matthias Van Bebber gave the Skippack settlers one hundred acres of land on which they might build a school and also bury the dead. It was to be used by all people in the community.

When Dock arrived in America he went immediately to the Skippack Creek settlement. The name *Skippack* means "ship's creek." He may already have been married, but he tells us nothing about his wife and family. From his last will we now know that he had two daughters: Margareth, who married Henry Strycker, and Catharin, who married Pieter Jansen. If he was married when he arrived, the neighbors of the Skippack undoubtedly helped him build a log house. An old document shows that he bought one hundred acres of land sometime before 1734. A lot of mystery surrounds his private life. He was very modest. He did not think it important to write about his own life.

MASTER DOCK'S SCHOOL

The Skippack settlers soon built a school on the land Mr. Van Bebber had given them. We do not know whether it was waiting for Master Dock when he arrived or whether they built it after he came. We do know that he began teaching in 1718, the same year in which he arrived.

There were no public schools in Pennsylvania at that time. Parents who wanted their children to receive an education paid a teacher, if they could find one, to teach them. Often they met in homes. If enough parents were interested they could together build a log school. Teachers often had very little training and were paid very little. Many did not seem to care about the children—except to punish them. They thought it was important for children to be afraid of their teacher so they would obey and learn their lessons. An average of ten or even twenty whippings a day was not uncommon for a school. Frequently those who had been whipped at school received another whipping from their parents at home in the evening. A favorite verse of many teachers was:

Students . . . like horses on a road,
Must be well lashed before they take
the load;

They may be willing for a time to run,
But you must whip them, ere the work be done.

Lesser punishments included twisting the nose, snapping the forehead, pulling the ears, or calling the culprits "dunce" or "blockhead" or "booby."

The pupils were not angels either. They evened the score with the teacher by a variety of tricks and pranks. The two favorite ones seem to have been locking the teacher out of the school and stuffing wet rags into the chimney so that when a fire was started the smoke would drive everybody out of the room.

Master Dock's school was different. He loved his pupils. Every evening, after they had gone home, he took the list of their names, knelt down at his desk, and prayed for them one by one. We can almost hear him pray, "And then there is Jimmy. O Lord, you know he is not a bad boy, but he always makes such mischief. Help me to teach him to be honest, and strong in heart. And Sarah. She is a good girl, dear God, but she talks too much. Help me to show her how to use her time better. . . ." Once he wrote: "I owe God particular thanks because besides calling me to this profession [teaching] He has given me an extreme love of children." He believed God wanted him to be a teacher.

There came a time when Master Dock left teaching and began to farm. We do not know why. It may be that he needed more money than he was receiving as a teacher. But after ten years he felt very guilty about it and came back to his school. He prayed God to forgive him and "overlook my neglect of youth" during the time he had farmed.

There was discipline in Master Dock's school, but only to help the pupils, not to make them afraid. He often rewarded them for good work. The younger children would receive a note to their parents saying, "Dear Mr. Brubacher: Amos has been a good boy. He has learned the ABC. Please give him one penny and two fried eggs. Christopher Dock." Older children received beautiful designs he had made, or were allowed to be his helpers for a day. The best pupils were allowed to read the Bible aloud for morning devotions at the school. On rare occasions they might be allowed to accompany him on a trip to Germantown.

Master Dock had a punishment bench on which guilty pupils had to sit. If someone was heard swearing, for example, Dock would say, "Who taught you those words?" It usually turned out to be an adult, and he would make a mental note to talk to that adult later. Then he would ask the pupil, "Do you understand what you were saying?" and explain it to him. If the pupil was sorry, he was given another chance. Should he swear a second time, he had to sit on the punishment bench with a yoke around his neck to show that he was guilty and caught in a bad habit. If nothing else helped, he was eventually whipped, but this did not happen often because the pupils loved their teacher and tried very hard to please him.

Because stealing was a constant temptation and quickly led to lying, Master Dock developed the following rule: "No child may give or exchange anything in school, on the way, or at home without first informing me or his parents. Even if he finds something in school, on the road, or wherever it may be, he is to tell me immediately. For what they find is not yet their property, but the loser's." If no loser claimed it, the finder was eventually able to keep it.

Master Dock wanted his children to

learn love and humility. If one of them pushed others to get ahead in a line he was sent to the end of the line and had to stay there for days and weeks until his behavior showed he was worthy of being moved higher. If a pupil daydreamed or failed to get his work done for other reasons he was eventually, after fair warnings, made to stand before the whole school, and the pupils all called out, "Lazy, lazy." If two pupils quarreled they had to sit together until they were

friends, and Master Dock said, "If this could happen so easily among adults, and if they could forgive and forget like children, then

> *By lawsuits no purses depleted would be,*
> *And lawyers would never grow rich on their fee.*
> *The nagging conscience would come to rest,*
> *With love and peace life would be blest;*
> *There would be much less ache and dole*
> *For body and soul."*

Master Dock also had a rule "For Stopping Chattering and Restoring Silence." If the class was restless, a monitor was appointed to stand on a bench and watch every pupil. The names of offenders were written on the board. If they were quiet then, all was well. If not, they were made to sit on the punishment bench. There, Master Dock wrote, "they are given their choice, whether they prefer to wear the yoke or receive a rap on the hand. They seldom choose the yoke but usually hold out their hands to the rod."

The worst offense a pupil could commit was to lie. The first time it happened, Master Dock would have a long discussion with the child, pointing out that the devil himself is the father of lies (Jn. 8:44). The second offense led to a sound whipping. Often bondsmen were appointed. These were trusted pupils who volunteered to help the culprit to reform his habits. The worse the offense, the more bondsmen might be required, except for lying. Then no bondsman could help. Before he talked or disciplined a lying pupil Master Dock always, he wrote, offered "a sincere and ardent prayer to God for aid and support." It was a very serious sin in his eyes.

Children who moved into the community often hated to go to school. It was much more fun, they thought, to roam through the woods and fish in the streams and Skippack Creek. But after the first day of school most of them were glad to return. It was fun to play together and to learn to read and write. Master Dock had interesting ways of doing things, too. The following, for example, is his own description of how children were allowed to leave the room for the toilet, which was, of course, outdoors: "Children find it necessary to ask to leave the building, and this must be permitted if one does not want to have filth and stench in the school. But at times the cry for permission to leave the school continues all day even without need, so that at times two or three spend some time outside playing. To prevent this, I have driven a nail in the doorpost on which a little wooden hook is hung. The pupil who has to go out looks to see whether the hook is hanging beside the door. If it is there, it is a pass by which he may leave without asking; he simply takes the hook and goes out. If another has to go, he does not need to ask either, but stands in the doorway. As soon as the hook comes, he takes it from the other and goes out. If the hook stays away too long, and the case becomes urgent for the one in the doorway, he indicates this. Then I ask who was out last; he will know who received the pass from him; thus none can stay out too long."

Master Dock enjoyed singing, and sometimes wrote songs for the children. One of these songs has twenty-four stanzas. Another song had only five stanzas, of which two went as follows:

O children who are loving,
Be sure you love aright;
Find joy in ever moving
Toward heaven's radiant light.
Let love of God arise
To praise Him in the skies:
The virtue in such loving
Is heaven's highest prize.

Let us with voices ringing
Now swell the angel choir;
With shouting and with singing
New praise and love inspire!
We'll enter Zion's height
All in our shepherd's sight,
And dwell with Him forever
In everlasting light.

RULES OF CONDUCT FOR A CHILD AT SCHOOL

Soon Master Dock's name was known all over Pennsylvania as a good teacher. People were interested in knowing how he taught school. Christopher Sauer, a printer, admired Master Dock's work. He wanted to print a description of it in his paper, but he suspected Dock might say no. So he wrote to Dielman Kolb, a minister in the Mennonite church on the Skippack, and asked for his help. Minister Kolb responded by visiting Master Dock.

"Brother Dock," he said, "you have been doing a fine work in school for many years now. Would you be willing to write down how you do it? It would be so interesting for us to read."

"No," Master Dock replied, "that would only make me proud and eager for honor. It is better left unsaid."

"But would not your description be of great help to other teachers?" Minister Kolb asked.

They had a long discussion. Finally Master Dock said, "Well, I will do it, on two conditions."

"And what are they?" Minister Kolb asked.

"They are, first, that all glory be given to God, not to myself; and, second, that it not be printed until after I am dead."

Meanwhile, the printer Sauer died. Twenty years later, when Master Dock was an old man, the printer's son wanted to print the manuscript but could not find it. A notice was placed in his paper asking anyone who might have seen it to notify him, but no one came forward. Master Dock was glad and sent word to the young printer, "It is better so." But a year later it was found in the printing office, in a place where they had often looked for it before. It was printed with the consent of Master Dock. The name of Master Dock would probably be only a legend today if the manuscript had not been found.

Included in his writings were two hundred rules for children, teaching them how to behave at home, at school, on the street, in church, and everywhere. Among these are found the following rules for children at school:

"Dear child, when you enter the school, bow respectfully, and taking your place quietly, think of the presence of God.

"Always be obedient to your teacher and do not cause him to remind you of the same thing many times.

"If you are not asked, keep quiet and do not prompt others. Let them speak and answer for themselves.

"Toward your fellows act lovingly and peacefully; do not quarrel with them, hit them, dirty their clothes with your shoes or ink, nor give them nicknames. Act toward them always as you would have them act toward you.

"Avoid all improper, vulgar habits or actions at school. Such as, (1) Stretching with laziness the hands or the whole body. (2) Eating fruit or other things in school. (3) Leaning one's hand or arm on a neighbor's shoulder, leaning the head on the hand or laying it on the desk. (4) Putting one's feet on the bench or letting them dangle or scrape, crossing the legs or spreading them too far apart in sitting or standing. (5) Scratching the head. (6) Playing with the fingers or chewing them. (7) Turning the head in all directions. (8) Sitting and sleeping. (9) Crawling under benches or desks. (10) Turning the back upon the teacher.

"Keep your books clean inside and out; do not scribble or draw in them; do not lose or tear them.

"When school is out do not make a clatter. In going down stairs do not jump two or three steps at a time, lest you hurt yourself. Go quietly home."

In all these rules Master Dock's first concern was for the pupil. Rules were meant to help the pupil grow in knowledge and faith, not to be enforced for their own sake. They were a part of his love for children. They spoke to their inner needs and emotions.

"If an angry or revengeful thought tries to arise in thee, subdue it by the thought of the love and gentleness of Jesus Christ.

"Employ thy mouth to call for His help in trouble, to praise His love, and to thank Him for all His benefits.

"But so shape thy deeds also, that God may be glorified in them."

SCHOOL IS OUT

One evening in the fall of 1771 Master Dock did not return home. His wife had died long before and he was living with friends. They searched and called for him in the woods on the way to school but did not find him. When they came to the school they found him at his desk—dead. He had taught to the last hour of his life, and died while on his knees in prayer for his pupils, as was his custom. He was buried in the Skippack Mennonite Church cemetery, but the location of his grave was unknown for many years until the old gravestone was found again in 1958.

His last will was a final honor to God, whom he had served faithfully so many years. "I give and recommend my Soul," he wrote, "into the hands of God that gave it, and for my Body I recommend it to the Earth . . . nothing doubting but at the general Resurrection I shall receive the same again by the mighty Power of God." The will divided his property between his two daughters and their husbands, and added: "I ORDAIN further in this my last Will, that my Son in Law Henry Stryckers and my Son in Law Pieter Jansen . . . shall have no Power to Spoil any green Woods, Except to Reform the fence. . . ."

Not far from where the humble Master Dock lies buried, a living monument has been erected: the Christopher Dock Mennonite High School. Times have changed since he taught over two hundred years ago, but the need for love and faith and sound learning continues.

2

Johann Cornies
1789-1848

We must work the works of him who sent me, while it is day; night comes, when no one can work. JOHN 9:4

Freedom was in the air as the eighteenth century drew to a close. In America the thirteen colonies issued their Declaration of Independence in 1776. In England William Carey declared God was calling him to India as a missionary to set people free from superstition through faith in Christ. And in China the people longed to be free from the terrible effects of the drug opium, which the British were bringing into their country illegally.

In those days freedom also became real again to the Mennonites. In 1775, during the American Revolution, they wrote to their government, "We find no freedom in giving, or doing, or assisting in any thing by which men's lives are destroyed." A few years later they drew up the first petition against slavery in America. Far away in Germany, Mennonites began to emigrate to Russia in 1789 to find new land and avoid being drafted into the German army.

In that same year of 1789, a little boy was born into the Cornies home near Danzig on the Baltic Sea. His father was a sailor who loved his wife and home, but was usually far away sailing the stormy seas or loading precious cargo in some strange, exciting port. The baby's mother was a kind and beautiful woman. She was often lonely. But now she had a son to be with her and she would no longer be alone when her husband was gone. They named him Johann,

meaning John. Although they did not know it then, he too would be concerned for freedom. Through him many people would be set free from poverty and ignorance in the years to come.

As Johann grew older he sometimes went to school, but because his parents were poor they moved often. He hated to leave old friends and find his way in a new school with new, stern teachers. No one was made to go to school. Many children never went, but Johann wanted to learn to read and write. Most of all he wanted to study maps in order to find the places his father had told him about —Lisbon, Cape Town, Bombay, and Calcutta. Even his friends envied him for the stories he could tell and the souvenirs he could bring to class from Portugal, Africa, and India.

In time there were four boys in the Cornies family—Johann, Peter, David, and Henry. Sometimes their mother could hardly manage them by herself. One day Johann heard two neighbor women talking to each other, and one said, "That poor Frau Cornies. Have you ever seen such wild boys? They will be the death of her yet!" Of course they loved their mother, but they were boys and missed their daddy who was always far away.

ON TO RUSSIA

Suddenly everything changed. One evening, soon after their father had come home from another one of his long ocean

voyages, he called all four boys together and said, "Well, boys, I have news for you. How would you like it if I stayed home with you from now on?"

"Great!" they answered. "How long are you staying this time?"

"Always," he replied. "I won't go back to sea again. I want to stay home with you and mother."

"Yippee!" was all the boys could shout again and again. "Yippee! Yippee!"

Poor Mother thought they would raise the roof of the house with their shouting.

"But," Father Cornies said finally after order had been restored, "we cannot stay here. There is no work here for me. Mother and I have decided we will go to Russia, where Uncle Herman and Aunt Agathe are, and buy a farm. Shall we all be farmers?"

"Yes," they shouted eagerly, "we will all be farmers." And farmers they were to be indeed.

They did not have much to load. One wagon and a team of horses took all their belongings, but it was a long and weary road—one thousand lonely miles. Often the boys would walk or run behind the wagon, or go far ahead of it, just for fun. Winter had arrived by the time they came to the Chortitza Colony and so they stayed with friends.

But they needed money to start farming. Fortunately Father Cornies had an interesting and useful hobby. He was a chiropractor, a kind of self-trained doctor who could massage people's aching muscles and use all kinds of herbs from the flowers of the steppes to prepare medicines for them. Soon people came from far and near to have him help them. They called him "doctor." He hardly had time to start farming. Long after he died, his pioneer farm was still known to everybody as the doctor's farm.

Johann had also found a job. He worked in a huge mill which ground wheat into flour, but he did not like the noise of the grinders and the dusty, prickly chaff which fell on him all day long. One day, after he had worked there for a whole year, he said to Father Cornies, "Father, I don't want to be a miller all my life. I have saved most of my wages this past year. Will you lend me a little money so I can go into business on my own?"

"Well," his father replied, "I suppose so, but what kind of business do you have in mind? You're only sixteen years old."

"I know," Johann answered, as he began to explain his plans. He would buy butter and cheese, meat and vegetables from the Mennonite farmers and haul them to the cities of Sevastopol and Simferopol in the Crimea for resale at a profit.

"But," his father replied, "that is a trip of 150 miles, one way. The road is bad, especially in winter, and I have heard there are robbers, too."

"Don't you worry about me," Johann answered. "You will soon see that it will pay very well."

Johann was right. It became a very profitable business. But his father was right, too. It was a dangerous road. Since there was no bridge over the Sywash River Johann always loaded his wagon onto a boat, while he made the horses swim across. One day a sinister-looking Armenian trader became so angry at Johann that he threw him out of his warehouse and threatened to kill him. Johann picked himself up and went away, but when he counted his money he realized the trader had overpaid him. He turned right around and went back to the dark old warehouse and the angry trader and said, "You paid me too much. Here is your change."

And the old trader, no longer angry, replied, "I have never met an honest man like you."

One of the nicest rewards of his business, as far as Johann was concerned, was that the long wagon trips gave him time to read and to think. He seldom left home without a book about farming, or history, or about the church. People who did not know about this often wondered how Johann could be so well educated with the little schooling he had received in Germany.

LUCKA MALYJ

But Johann did not think only about his business and his books. More and more he found himself thinking, or dreaming, about Agnes Klassen, the girl he loved and hoped to marry. On a memorable day in the spring of 1811, when she was nineteen and he was twenty-two, they were married.

It was customary in those days for a young couple to live with the parents of the bridegroom for several years, and so Johann and Agnes moved into a large room of the "Doctor Cornies" home. At first all went well, but the second winter was very cold. It was the winter when over three hundred thousand of Napoleon's French soldiers froze to death in Russia. Because the barns were not warm enough Father Cornies and his hired men brought newborn calves and dozens of little lambs into the house to keep them from freezing. One day when Johann came home he found Agnes crying. The men had brought in a litter of piglets, too, and little Johann, Jr., who was only a few weeks old, had to live in the same room with all those squealing, baa-ing, and mooing little beasts.

"Johann," Agnes said with a strange look in her eyes, "I've had enough. You must get us out of here."

"Yes," he replied, "in spring we will build our own home."

The home which Johann built in the village of Orloff was by far the handsomest of any in the area. Though he was still a young man, he was no longer poor. He seemed to succeed at everything he tried, especially at sheep raising. To start his herd he bought 250 "scrubs" at a low price. Then he imported purebred Merino rams from Spain and improved the breed until their soft, white wool was considered the best in Russia.

One day a young man came to the Cornies farm. Agnes answered the door. "I am Lucka Malyj," he said in Russian. "I am a shepherd. Do you have work for me?"

As Agnes went to call Johann she whispered to him, "He is a good man. You should hire him."

Johann took her advice, as he often did, and never regretted it. Lucka served the Cornies family as chief shepherd of the sheep for over fifty years, long after Johann himself had died. Though he had many shepherds to help him, he seemed to know every sheep personally. Summer and winter, sun and rain, he was always with the sheep.

Lucka was sick only twice in his long life. Once he had a boil, and another time a toothache. He came to Johann's brother David, who had taken their father's place as "doctor," to have his aching tooth pulled. There were no dentists in those parts of the country. David took a big pair of pliers and began to pull with all his might, but the pliers slipped and Lucka was practically wild with pain. Without waiting for a second try he gave one big shout, jumped on his horse, and rode off. He said later that he never had a toothache after that. Unfortunately we do not know what happened to the half-pulled tooth.

With Lucka to help Johann the flock of sheep grew bigger and bigger. He rented nine thousand acres of government land to provide more pasture for them. Other shepherds had to remove their sheep from this land since it now belonged to Cornies.

One evening as he and a friend were riding across the land, far from home, to check on his sheep, they came upon a shepherd herding his own sheep on Johann's land. He was a wild-looking fellow, and Johann recognized him as a member of the nomadic Nogaier tribe.

After greeting him, Johann said, "I am very sorry, but this is my land. You will either need to pay me for pasturing your sheep here, or take them elsewhere."

The nomad became very angry and put his hand to his dagger; he argued and cursed and promised revenge, but Johann calmly waited for him to make up his mind. Finally the wild shepherd paid the amount Johann had asked. Then, just when Johann's friend thought they should get away as fast as possible, Johann said to the shepherd, "It is dark now, and our home is far away. May we stay in your tent for the night?"

"My tent is your tent," the shepherd replied and led them to it.

They visited as they ate meat by the fire. Then Johann rolled himself into a blanket and was soon sound asleep, but his friend lay wide-eyed with fear till morning. He was certain that the shepherd would murder them. He did not know, as Johann did, that according to nomadic tribal custom they would never be hurt as long as they were guests, even of their enemy. They were safer in his tent than if they had tried to ride home in the dark where he might indeed have tried to get them. In the morning Johann thanked him and they parted almost as friends.

YUSCHANLEE

Johann was not only a sheep rancher. On his farm in Orloff he experimented with new kinds of wheat and other grain. He planted the first fruit trees anyone had ever seen in that region. There were few trees of any kind on the wide open steppes, so Johann began a tree nursery on his farm and planted shelter belts. As he had improved his sheep breed, so he also bought purebred bulls from Holland and purebred horses of Arab stock.

Soon people began to visit his farm to see what he was doing and to ask his advice. He was very pleased to be able to help them, to sell them little trees or purebred stock, or just to talk with them about their problems. He loved the great outdoors and everything in it as a part of God's wonderful creation.

Slowly a new idea took shape in his mind. He would build a large experimental farm where all could receive the help they needed. One morning, after he had spent the night on his sheep ranch sleeping under the open sky, he found the spot for the experimental station in a beautiful valley on the banks of a little stream that ran through his ranch. He decided to name it Yuschanlee, after the stream itself.

Johann immediately set to work constructing the farm buildings, digging wells, planting trees, and finding the right workers to help him. There was so much to do that Agnes said, "Johann, you are working too hard."

But he replied, "No, Agnes, I am not. I am serving God and man. All nature is an open book about the love of God for each of us."

To a friend he wrote: "I feel the urge to work as much as is in my power, while it is day; for night is surely coming, when no one can work. My hope is not

steppes – vast semi-arid grass-covered plain.

in other people, nor do the criticisms of my opponents bother me. I have placed my confidence in God my Savior. Now is the time for us to work for Him. Do not become discouraged; let us go forward in the name of our Lord."

By now Johann was a famous man. The government appointed him as permanent chairman of the Russian Agricultural Society for south Russia. All farmers had to follow his advice or be punished by the government as lawbreakers. Most of them were very thankful for his help, but some were jealous. Johann was too powerful and too rich for them.

One day Johann received a letter from a man in a distant village. "The trees you sent me do not grow here," he wrote. "Those from last year died, too. We cannot grow trees in this part of the country."

As soon as he could, Johann drove out to the village. "Here," the man said, "look at this tree, and this one, and this one. None of your trees are growing."

Johann did not say a word. He was very angry. The man had planted all the trees with their tips in the ground and the roots in the air to spite him and make fun of his work. Because of this the court sentenced the man to be whipped, and the church expelled him from membership. This made him so angry at Johann and the church that he never went back to church, except for the funeral of his wife, though he lived for another thirty years.

Because Yuschanlee was so successful as a model farm, Johann bought a second tract of land in another community, and later a third tract until he farmed over twenty-five thousand acres of land in his three model farms. He introduced the idea of crop rotation and summer fallow to the farmers. He showed them

how to grow new crops like flax and tobacco and corn. He introduced silkworms. In order to feed them, he planted three hundred thousand mulberry trees. This, in turn, gave work to thousands of people who spun the silk. He built dams and showed farmers how to irrigate dry land. He was particularly successful in growing good potatoes. Cheese made under his direction was soon in great demand even for export to other countries. Every year he published a statement of the income and expenses from each farm so that farmers knew exactly whether good farming paid off or not.

In spite of this success Johann remained an humble man. One day Czar Alexander I, the king of Russia, and his young son visited Johann in his own home. They honored him with praise and gifts, but Johann said, "I just want to be a simple, honest Mennonite farmer."

Soon after the visit Johann received an official letter from the Czar's office asking him whether he would take young men as farm trainees on his model farms. He replied: "I will take sixteen Russian and Nogaier young men between the ages of fifteen and seventeen years. The course of study will take from four to six years, depending on their progress. . . . The students will be taught and supported at my expense. The request of the government that they also learn to read and write will be met." Soon Johann arranged for other good Mennonite farmers to take trainees also. Agnes began by taking four girls into her home to teach them how to sew, cook, read, and write. When the young men graduated they went all over Russia to establish model farms of their own, with the help of Johann and the government. Others came to take their place year after year.

Johann was particularly happy to

work with the government in settling the wild, nomadic Nogaiers in agricultural communities. They were the proud descendants of the great conqueror Ghengis Khan, but they soon learned to trust Johann. They called him *white-eye.* He spoke their language, ate their food, and drank their horse milk. In time he helped to settle seventeen thousand of them on farms. At the request of the government Johann also helped Jewish, Swedish, and Hutterite settlers with their problems.

The Hutterites were cousins of the Mennonites, but did not live near them. Often Hutterite parents decided whom their sons and daughters should marry. One day a pretty young Hutterite girl came to Johann and Agnes.

"My parents," she cried, "want me to marry an old widower with nine children, and I won't."

"Why, don't you love him?" Johann asked.

"No," she replied, "I don't."

"Do you love somebody else then?" he asked.

"No, I don't," she responded blushing, "but I won't marry that man."

"Well," Johann said softly to Agnes, "what do we do now?"

Agnes answered, "You cannot let them make her unhappy for the rest of her life."

So Agnes gave the young girl work in her own home, and Johann had a good talk with her parents. He also wrote a decree that no marriages could henceforth take place unless the couple first signed a statement saying they were marrying each other of their own free will. The young people loved him for that.

Better Schools and Happy Children

"Do you know that our schools are terrible?" Johann said one day to the members of the Agricultural Society of which he was chairman. "We must do something about them."

"But we are an agricultural society," they replied. "What do we know about schools? And besides, that is the work of the church; the ministers will never let us change the schools."

"We will wait and see," Johann said softly as he dismissed the meeting.

The schools were indeed terrible. Most teachers had no training except what they had received in the same schools when they were young. All classes met together in the home of the teacher. There were no grades and few books besides the Bible. Teachers often whipped their pupils or hit them over the head or boxed their ears without good cause. Whether they attended school at all or were kept at home to work was the parents' decision. Often the children were afraid of the teacher and of school.

Soon every teacher in the settlement received a letter from Johann describing conditions as he often found them in his visits to these schools.

"The teacher," he wrote, "sits in his miserable shack with his pupils in the same room in which he lives with his wife and children. He is still wearing his white linen nightshirt and soiled nightcap. He has a pipe in his mouth. Before him on the table lie a few dirty books, together with straps and other instruments of punishment. The pupils stand around the table without being grouped according to age, size, or ability. The walls are covered with hammers, saws, pots and pans, and everything the family owns. Old stockings, pants, and other laundry hangs around the stove. The baby in the cradle cries until one of the pupils is finally ordered to rock it to sleep. A hen with chickens and several pigeons walk and fly around among the children.

"Because of this," the letter continued, "the pupils find it difficult to pay attention to the teacher. They fuss and shove and tease each other constantly. This makes the teacher very angry. He begins to shout at them, then he curses and swears; he hangs heavy objects around their necks, makes them kneel on wood or dried peas, boxes their ears, and hits them on the mouth. And all the while he thinks he is keeping order and discipline."

A favorite text of many teachers in those days was taken from Sirach, a book sometimes included in the Bible: "Bow down his neck in his youth, and beat his sides while he is young, lest he become stubborn and disobey you, and you have sorrow of soul from him" (30: 12). They believed they were doing the will of God in obeying this text.

How could Johann change all this? He began by building a school to train teachers. As soon as he had enough replacements the older incompetent teachers were told to find other work. He raised money to build schools in the villages and to pay the teachers. He ordered textbooks from Germany and put some of his best teachers to work building a curriculum which included the following subjects:

1. Bible study
2. Reading (both silent and oral)
3. Writing (including spelling and dictation)
4. Recitation and composition
5. Arithmetic (written and mental)
6. Geography
7. Penmanship
8. Singing
9. Recitation of memory work
10. Reading from the Bible

School attendance was made compulsory. Parents who kept their children home for no good reason had to pay a fine. Finally, with the help of others, Johann drew up a list of eighty-eight rules for teachers to follow. Rule 40, for example, read: "If a teacher would have his pupils enjoy their studies, he must show that he himself enjoys them and that he loves to teach."

Not everybody liked these changes. Some wanted things to be the way they had always been. Johann started libraries in the villages so parents could keep up with their children, but those who did not like his work also did not like to read. And Johann could be very firm; his opponents called him stubborn. One of them wrote later, "As Cornies became rich and famous his heart grew hard and cold." Things usually had to go his way. Once his enemies dug a huge "bear trap" pit right in the path where Johann often rode in his fields, put sharp sticks into it and covered it with branches and grass, hoping he would fall into it and be killed. But his faithful sandy-yellow horse sensed the danger and jumped aside. Johann never found out who had done it.

One of the leading ministers of the church was particularly opposed to Johann's work. Johann had helped organize support for the British and Foreign Bible Society which was distributing Bibles in Russia. The minister thought that was bad. Johann just had too much authority, he thought. And now these changes in the schools were the last straw. He packed his bag and traveled to faraway Odessa to report Johann to the government as an enemy of the people. When he returned he said to all who would listen, "The government will investigate Cornies, and has already decided to exile him to slave labor in Siberia."

But when men came to investigate the charges, they soon saw the truth. Not Johann, but the minister was found guilty. He was ordered to stop preaching. His huge congregation was divided into three congregations, and each one of these elected a new, progressive leader.

A BROKEN SHAFT

One day in the spring of 1848, in the midst of all his work, Johann became seriously ill. Agnes had died a year earlier. He was lonely. His son, Johann, Jr., and daughter, Agnes, were both visiting far away in Germany. When someone said, "It's too bad your children are not here with you now," Johann calmly replied, "Leave them where they are. They could not help me now anyway."

He had been in bed for over a week. There was little the doctor seemed to be able to do to help him. Suddenly he got up and said, "Help me get dressed. I want to go outside."

He dressed completely, even putting on his riding boots. Then he went outside. But he did not go far; he simply stood in front of his house and gazed in-

tently around him at the beauty of nature which he had loved so much and taken as a gift from the hand of God. He sighed and made one farewell motion with his hand. Then he returned to bed. There he died a few days later, just after he had told his friend and minister Peter Neufeld how gracious God had been to him all his life.

A large number of people came to his funeral. They said many fine things about all the great achievements of Johann's full and active life. But no one put it better than his friend Peter Neufeld when he said, "Johann Cornies was a wonderful gift of God to the Mennonite people." His two children and his many friends erected a monument at his grave a year later. It was a broken shaft—to symbolize that the work he had begun was not finished. Others would need to carry on. And they did.

3

John H. Oberholtzer
1809-1895

The fear of the Lord is the beginning of wisdom. PSALM 111:10

The story of John H. Oberholtzer takes us back to the days when Abraham Lincoln was president of the United States. It takes us back to the time of the Civil War and the underground railroad by which slaves escaped from their southern masters to freedom in Canada. Neither the automobile nor the radio had yet been invented, but the first telephone conversation over a line two miles long took place on October 9, 1876, when John Oberholtzer was sixty-seven years old.

Very little is known about John's boyhood years. We know he was born on January 10, 1809, on a farm near Clayton in Berks County, Pennsylvania. Since his mother's maiden name was Susanna Hunsberger, his parents called him John Hunsberger Oberholtzer. His father's name was Abram. His great-grandfather, Jacob Oberholtzer, had come to America in 1732 as a young widower with two little children.

There were no public schools in America early in the nineteenth century, but some people had private schools and admitted pupils who could pay a fee. There were also church schools like the one Master Dock had taught at Skippack. It is likely that John attended a school like this because he became very interested in books and education. Schools were open only during the winter months. We can imagine John enjoying the great outdoors during the summer days, perhaps fishing, or playing ball with his friends, or helping with the farm chores. He may have had his own riding horse or some calves to feed, but if he did, we do not know about it.

We do know that he did not become a farmer. Perhaps he did not like farming. He must have been a good student, for by the time he was sixteen he was a schoolteacher himself!

THOSE BOYS!

Teacher John has his troubles with some of the boys. The school was owned by John Ritter who had built it for his sons and had hired John as teacher. Other pupils were also admitted. Since only the top floor of the building was needed for classes, John Ritter, who was a farmer, put pigs on the first floor. Unfortunately, the sons of Mr. Ritter demanded much attention from John because the school was at their home and their father owned it. But John could not spend all of his time only with them. Consequently, when they became angry or tired or bored, they would go downstairs and stir the feed barrel which immediately brought all the pigs running and squealing because they thought they would be fed. And when they did not get fed they kept up their squealing and grunting until the school had to be dismissed because of all the noise and dust and smell. This became such a problem that John finally resigned and moved to another school. He continued teaching for sixteen years.

School was in session only during the winter months so John needed to find employment for the summer. He enjoyed making things with his hands. Locks fascinated him. But there were no factories to make them. He immediately saw an opportunity. Soon he was a one-man lock factory with a small shop in his house in Milford Square. No lock seemed to be too big or too small for him to tackle. Some of the locks he made are still in use in the community, including a large one in the door of the Flatland Mennonite Church. It was a profitable business, too. He supported his family with it later, together with his teaching, and had money for many other good causes.

Before long John was an established and respected member of the community. He was baptized and united with the Mennonite Church at Great Swamp. He married Mary Bean. Two children were born to them, David in 1834 and Anna two years later.

A CALL FROM GOD

The minister of the Great Swamp church was over eighty years old by the time John was thirty-three, and needed help. In those days congregations usually had several ministers. They served part-time, and without pay. To find a new minister the churches used the lot. The congregation would write the names of persons they believed would make good ministers on a piece of paper and hand it in to the leading minister or bishop. At a special meeting the bishop would then call the men who had been nominated to come forward and pick up one Bible from the row of Bibles he had placed on a front bench. There were always just as many Bibles as men nominated, but one had a slip in it which usually said, "The lot is cast into the lap, but the decision is wholly from the Lord." This was a quote from Proverbs 16:33. The person who picked up the Bible with the slip in it was the new minister. It was believed that God himself was able to choose the right man in that way.

One day Samuel Musselman, the old minister of John's church, asked the members to write down names of men they wished to nominate for the ministry. Fifteen names were handed in, John's among them. He was not at all certain that the lot method was the right way to choose a minister. He thought some of the ministers chosen in that way were not suited for the work, but he did not know how he could change it. On the appointed day the men came forward to choose their Bibles. When John opened his, the lot was in it. It would have been almost impossible to refuse it because the church believed this was God himself calling him to service. So John became a minister in the Franconia Conference.

One Sunday morning, about six weeks later, as John walked into church, Samuel Musselman said to him, "John, would you like to preach today?"

It was believed that a minister should always be prepared to preach, without having time for preparation, and that the Holy Spirit would give him the right words to speak. "Alright," said John, "I will, with God's help."

"As I knelt in prayer before the sermon," he wrote later, "I cried to God, poor sinner that I am, and asked in all humility that He would support me by His grace. Since it was now my duty to preach, I asked for courage not to be afraid to proclaim faithfully His will and counsel. . . . And what happened? While I was praying the verse from Hebrews

13:5 came to my mind, 'I will never fail you nor forsake you . . . .' I knew this was an answer to prayer and received courage to preach on the text, 'For by grace you have been saved, through faith . . .' " (Eph. 2:8, 9).

Not everyone liked his sermon. As he walked out John heard someone say, "That was a scholarly sermon," which meant that it had been bad because being a scholar meant being proud. Pride was the ancient sin of Adam and Eve in the garden of Eden and the big temptation for all men. He knew immediately that his new ideas and enthusiasm would not be welcomed by some people in the church.

The years before John became a minister had been difficult for the Mennonites in Pennsylvania. Many changes had come to America without affecting them a great deal because they lived in closed communities among themselves. The War of Independence had caused some to emigrate to Ontario by 1800 because they wanted to remain loyal to England and King George III, but most of them continued farming as before. Some were quite wealthy. New spiritual life came to many churches through revival meetings, but the Mennonites did not allow *outsiders* into their churches. Other churches were sending out missionaries, but not the Mennonites. Other Christian young people were attending colleges and universities, but Mennonite young people were not allowed to do this because their elders thought it would make them proud and destroy their faith in Christ. God did not change and the Bible did not change. Why should the church change?

This attitude made John impatient. "Abram," he said one day to his friend Abram Hunsicker, "we must help our church to change. We are not faithful to the way of Jesus. Our young people do not care about the church anymore. What can we do?"

"Well, John," Abram replied, "we have talked about all this before. Give them an education, I say. Teach them to know what the Bible is really saying. Help our people to see what is important to believe and what is not important."

John knew he was right. He thought of the problem he was having with his suit coat. People were making a big issue of it. As a minister he was expected to wear a coat without a collar as a witness to faith and humility, but he had not yet bought one. Just the other day Samuel Musselman had said, "John, when are you getting your new coat?"

John had replied, "When this one is worn out."

He knew that was the wrong thing to say. The coat *was* worn out. He just didn't want to get a minister's coat. But to make matters worse he had added, "But tell me, Brother Musselman, why is the kind of coat I wear so important? I find nothing about it in the Bible."

Perhaps he had been too stubborn and too impatient. He knew some people were objecting more to his attitude than to his coat, but he could not help feeling he was right. "Will more education make it easier in the church?" he asked himself. And then he thought, "Even if it does, it will take a long time."

Fortunately he soon received a letter from Daniel Hoch in Ontario, to whom he had written about starting a Sunday school in the church. Daniel sent him a small catechism which had come from Germany. John could hardly wait to show it to his friend Abram. "Look," he said as he held the little book before him, "a guide to the study of the Bible." They began to read it together eagerly.

"Question: Which is the best book?

"Answer: The Bible.

"Q. Why?

"A. Because it tells us what God expects of us.

"Q. What does the word 'Bible' mean?

"A. It means: a book; but it always means the Holy Bible.

"Q. How do we know that it is the Word of God?

"A. It tells us things which only God knows."

So it continued, question after question, about Moses and Israel and the covenant of God.

"Abram," John said finally, "we must have this printed in many copies and start teaching it to the children of our church."

Soon children came to the Great Swamp Church every Sunday afternoon to study the Bible together with the new minister, John Oberholtzer. It was the first Mennonite Sunday school in America.

A few years later John wrote to friends in Germany about his work. "Now I will tell you how it used to be in our church when a new member asked to be admitted. If someone asked to join the church an announcement was made of this and others were invited to join, too. They would meet together with the minister once or twice. They were admonished to live right. Then they were baptized . . . without asking them whether they understood the meaning of salvation at all. They were not asked about that. . . . Now no one is received before we know that they are truly ready to witness to their faith in life and conduct. . . .

"We now have several places where Sunday school is being held, always in the afternoons when we have morning worship, which is every two weeks. When the children arrive (in some congregations there are sixty to seventy children enrolled, and even more) they first sing for half or three-quarters of an hour. Then a minister has a prayer. Then the children recite what they have memorized during the past two weeks. They are divided into classes. Many little children have already memorized the entire catechism, and many are memorizing parts of the Bible. . . . Adults from the congregation help, because it is too much for the minister alone. . . . We can see already that God is blessing this work. I hardly know where to stop writing. . . ."

BAD FEELINGS

Many people were very grateful for what John was doing to help the church, but some thought all the changes would destroy it. They felt he had too many non-Mennonite friends. He visited non-Mennonite churches and even preached from their pulpits. There were rumors that he had accepted money for that preaching, which meant he was selling the gospel to make money for himself. He was willing to admit Mennonites who had married non-Mennonites, and even their partners, into the church without rebaptizing them. Should not the church defend the faith against these things?

One day the older leaders of the church met and told John that unless he did as they, the church, said, he would need to leave their church. This was a hard blow, though he had expected it.

"But," he replied, "the church includes all the members, not just the ministers. Let us talk about it in the congregations."

Nevertheless, bad feelings continued on both sides. Both sides loved God and believed they were right, but both sides did wrong when they stopped loving each other.

Before long John thought he had an answer to their problems. He wrote a church constitution, which he called an *Ordnung*, which spelled out the duties and responsibilities of all people in the church, including ministers. It also asked that careful minutes be kept of each meeting in order that old questions need not be decided over and over again. The whole congregation, instead of the minister alone, would make all decisions. But all this was just another change which his opponents were unwilling to make. They told John and his friends that they were no longer in the church, but that they would be received back if they repented. John did not feel like repenting. He wanted to help the church become more faithful to Jesus.

Would love win out in the end? Many people tried to help. On October 5, 1848, a year after the break, John and his friends sent an "Offer of Peace" to their opponents, offering to meet with them to study what the gospel had to say to the issues between them, but the break remained. There were too many hard feelings and bad attitudes involved. There was also the problem of age. All but two of the ministers with John were under forty, while most of the ministers on the other side were much older. And so one-fourth of the members in the conference, five hundred in all, left the Franconia Conference to form sixteen congregations in a new conference which they called the East Pennsylvania Conference of the Mennonite Church. John's heart was heavy. He had prayed for unity and had reaped disunity. But he knew that God could use even this to bring glory to His name.

Unfortunately, these were not the only breaks in fellowship which John experienced. It took many years before the new conference became one family in Christ. Soon after the first break in 1847, a group in his church wanted to allow members to belong to secret societies, but John and the others felt there should be nothing done in secret in the church and that Christ alone should be Lord. So the group left.

A few years later the churches were troubled by new ways of preaching and witnessing in the community by men who wanted to awaken Mennonites and others from a long spiritual sleep. At first John supported these meetings, but he soon saw that they became a deep source of trouble in every church and family. It was decided that churches in his conference should not participate in them. This meant there could be no church prayer meetings either. "Christians should always be in prayer," John said. "I find nothing in the Bible about calling special meetings for prayer." And so another small group left and formed what was then called the Evangelical Mennonite Conference.

Still another small group asked why church members did not wash each other's feet at the communion service. They read John 13:15 where Jesus said, after He had washed the feet of His disciples, "I have given you an example, that you also should do as I have done to you." Then they asked, "Why don't we do that in our church?" John and the others said, "We cannot obey every verse in the Bible literally; we need to see its *spiritual* meaning." But the group believed that if the Bible said it they should do it, and left the new conference in 1859.

John was often troubled about these divisions. He wondered whether he himself lacked the right love for others. "I know that I, as every human being, am full of shortcomings and weaknesses," he wrote, "from which I daily need God's help increasingly to cleanse myself."

In sermons and talks he often said, "We must learn to repent; we must let the Holy Spirit lead us on." Surely divisions among brothers was not the will of God. And slowly new love and strength came to the group under John's steady hand.

JOHN BUYS A PRINTING PRESS

Now John worked harder than ever to increase the number of Sunday school classes in the congregations. He took a new interest in young people and encouraged them to continue their education. But another concern kept growing in his mind: should the church not have a mission and witness program to tell others about the gospel? Had Jesus not said, "Go, and make disciples of all nations . . ."?

"Mary," he said to his wife one day, "I am going to buy a printing press."

"A printing press?" she asked. "You alone? What for?"

And John replied, "To unite the Mennonites, to give them good literature to read, and to encourage them to do missionary work among non-Christians."

"Do you have the money?" she asked.

"I think we can manage," he answered. "It will cost up to four hundred dollars, but if I manage it right it should soon pay for itself."

And so the first Mennonite paper in America was born. John called it the *Religioeser Botschafter,* which meant *The Religious Messenger.* For his motto he chose a text from Psalm 111:10 that had always meant much to him: "The fear of the Lord is the beginning of wisdom." When the first issue appeared on August 23, 1852, the price was announced as seventy-five cents per year if paid in advance, and eighty-seven cents if paid at the end of the year. Now the scattered Mennonites could read about what was happening to their friends and relatives and other churches. They had good sermons and Bible studies right in their homes when the

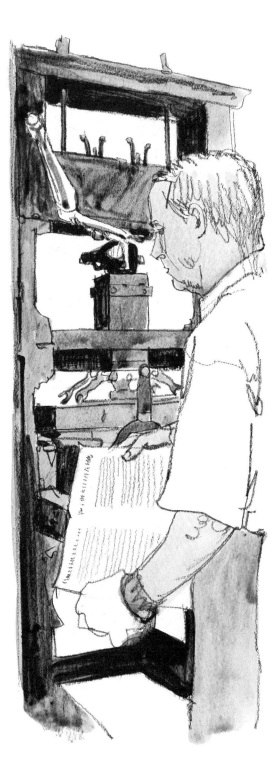

paper came. And often they were reminded of their responsibility for witnessing. For instance, John would write, "It is in order here to ask all our readers—have we fulfilled our responsibility for the conversion of the heathen?"

But John was not content with his achievement. "Abram," he would say to his friend, "if a small paper is good for our people to read, a good book would be even better."

Soon he announced that he intended to print a book of 505 pages by Gottfried Arnold on *Spiritual Experience.* He decided to publish it in parts. "One part of no less than seventy-two pages," he wrote, "will be published every six weeks, on good white paper together with paper cover for fifteen cents." He was able to proceed as planned until the entire book was published. It had a deep impact on the spiritual life of its readers. But it was also more than John's bank account could afford, and threatened to end his printing career.

His friends did not allow that to happen. They formed a company, gave the old paper a new name, *Das Christliche Volksblatt* (A Christian Paper for the People), and printed the first issue on July 30, 1856, only six months after the first paper had ended. Since most of the readers were farmers it carried many items of special interest to them, like the following:

Marks of a Good Milk Cow and Good Milk

A cow whose skin and tail is thin, whose tail joints are loose and far apart, whose large milk vein extends up to the front and divides into little crooked veins will produce much milk if she is fed and cared for properly. . . . On the other hand, a cow with a thick tail and short, thick tail joints only grows fat and produces little milk. . . .

The generally recognized characteristics of good milk are that it looks quite white and not blue . . . that it tastes and smells sweet, and when a drop is dropped on a fingernail or a plate it remains round and beautiful as a pearl. . . .

In the issue dated September 22, 1858, John reported the capture of a slave ship with 318 slaves on board. According to American law the captors were to receive one-half of the value of the ship and twenty-five dollars for each slave liberated. The slaves were to be sent back to Africa.

Two years later, on February 8, 1860, John urged the printing of tracts to use in evangelism. "Brethren," he wrote, "what shall we do? Shall we remain idle or shall we move forward? Shall we bury the talent the Lord has given us, or shall we invest it and use it . . . ?" He offered to produce and print a new tract in large quantity for every fifty dollars sent to him for this purpose.

John must have been either a very busy man or a forgetful one, as the following note in the May 15, 1861, issue indicates: "On May 2nd at the Council meeting at Deep Run a brother gave me two dollars for a subscription to the *Volksblatt;* and since I did not write it down immediately, I forgot who gave it to me. Who was it? . . . Please be patient and everything will be in order soon."

John was particularly grateful for the encouragement he received in his Sunday school work from John F. Funk, a young Mennonite businessman in Chicago, who was working with children in Dwight L. Moody's church. On November 27, 1861, Funk wrote, "The school was organized in a German neighborhood in the northwestern part of the city, away out almost on the prairie. . . . When it was first opened, there seemed to be little or no regard for the Christian religion . . . there was no religious service and no church or meetinghouse. . . ." But after having worked in the area for a time, Funk reported, "A number of parents have been induced, through the influence of their children, to read a chapter in the Bible and pray with their families every morning and evening, thus establishing a family altar . . . where seldom, if ever before, the voice of prayer had been heard."

This was also the time of the Civil War. The southern states were fighting to leave the Union and to continue slavery, while the North wanted to preserve the unity and put an end to slavery. John was against the South. In the May 14, 1862, issue of the *Volksblatt,* he printed a strong sermon by an unknown author, not himself, against the secession of the South from the Union. "This is an old teaching," the sermon writer declared. "It was taught many years ago. Lucifer [the devil] and his helpers acknowledged it. Because they could not rule they decided to secede and erect a confederation. 'Better to reign in hell than to serve in heaven,' spoke the President of that secession government."

His new friend, John F. Funk, continued to write from Chicago and send reports about the war. "We are looking with a great deal of anxiety to the movement of our army," he wrote on January 14, 1862, "and it has been reported within the last few days that a large number of troops have embarked from St. Louis to Cairo and Birds Point, from where the great army of from fifty thousand to sixty thousand men is to start southward, and sweep the wicked rebellion before it. . . . We hope their march will be a triumphant and successful one, and that soon we may hail with joy the return of peace. . . ."

Several months later he wrote another letter, saying: "Our city is, at present, in a high state of excitement on account of the call of the President [Lincoln] for three hundred thousand more troops . . . . Our ministers are preaching war sermons, and encouraging the people to come forward, and enlist . . . even in the house of God." Both John H. Oberholtzer and John F. Funk were deeply concerned about their nation and the outcome of the war.

One day, as the Confederate troops of General Robert E. Lee were preparing for what became the Battle of Gettysburg in July of 1863, the city of Chambersburg was burned to the ground. This was a signal to John that help was needed immediately. Partly through his efforts large sums of money were raised and supplies gathered for the unfortunate citizens of the city.

A CONFERENCE IS BORN

During all these years the longing for unity had grown stronger and stronger in John's heart. He wrote about it in his paper, preached about it, and prayed about it. He knew that Mennonites would need to work together if they hoped to build good schools and send out missionaries. But the division with the Franconia Conference continued and the small groups that had left his conference had not returned. Some people called his East Pennsylvania Conference the "New" Mennonites, and the conference they had left the "Old" Mennonites.

One day early in 1860 he received for publication in the *Volksblatt* the minutes of a conference three congregations in Iowa had held the year before. Included in the minutes was an invitation to all others who might be interested to attend the next meeting on "the second day of Pentecost in 1860 at West Point |Iowa|." John did not have the money to go, but at the last minute friends raised enough, and he went.

It was a small conference. Only four visitors came. One of them was John. Five sermons were preached before they turned to business, but the things they then discussed made him deeply grateful. They had five concerns. First, the need to form a missionary society; second, the need to form a historical society to help them understand themselves; third, the need for a Christian school to train missionaries and church workers; and fourth, the need for more tracts for evangelism on city streets.

The fifth concern was for unity. "How can we as Mennonite churches work together and yet each keep our freedom?" they asked. A committee was appointed to develop a plan of union, and when it reported next day the plan was adopted. The congregations agreed to work together in missions and education without destroying the freedom of any one of them to do things on their own. And so here, in a little town in Iowa, with only a small number of churches represented, the General Conference Mennonite Church was born. It was simply a decision of the churches represented to work together in the things they knew God wanted them to do. John was elected chairman of the new conference. He returned home with a grateful heart.

In the September 5, 1860, issue of the *Volksblatt* he reported on his experience: "The West Point conference, which was held at Pentecost, was not without significance. Not without significance were the many and heartfelt prayers which ascended to the throne of grace. . . . If the seed which was planted

there is good, then, if the Lord adds His blessing, it will bring forth fruit in its time — who knows — thirtyfold or even fortyfold."

And fruit did come. Soon Daniel Hege was appointed to visit all the scattered families in Ontario, the Midwest, Ohio, and Pennsylvania. A young man in Canada volunteered as a missionary, and plans were made to build a school in Wadsworth, Ohio. But progress was slow because the people were not used to having the church support so much work. One of the excuses John often heard was that they had to save their money for the draft. Finally John wrote in the *Volksblatt,* "People say, 'I can't give the money now, because I do not know whether I will be drafted or not; I must keep it to buy my freedom in case I am drafted . . . .' " Then John admonished his readers that God had called the church to this work and that "where there is a will there is also a way." The school was built and classes began on January 2, 1868.

DAVID AND MARY

Though John was happy and grateful to God for progress in the work of the church, another heavy burden weighed upon him—the life of his son David. David was an intelligent and likeable young man, but he did not care to work and he fell into bad habits. After a time he married, but could not get along with his wife and sometimes left her alone with their two children. When the Civil War came he enlisted in the army and never returned. Some people said, "How can John be a minister of a church if he cannot even care for his own family?"

One day an old man told John he had seen David in New York City and that he was a printer there. John knew that this would be possible since David had learned the printer's trade from him as a boy. John took the train to New York to find him. He visited one printshop after another, he asked for him everywhere, he prayed, and he waited. But he found no trace of him. Perhaps he had died in the war without being reported.

One day John's wife Mary died, and he was left alone. After a time he married a widow, Susanna Moyer, who came from the Swamp community but now lived in Philadelphia. She returned to her old home with him, but since she did not like it he moved back to Philadelphia with her. There he soon grew homesick for the country. The busy city streets were just too much for him, and so he spent much time living with relatives and old friends in his home community while Susanna stayed in the city. He longed for the warmth and love of a close family, but was often alone. In spite of it all, his faith remained firm. Had the Lord not promised, "I will never fail you nor forsake you"?

FATHER OBERHOLTZER

As John became older, friends began to refer to him as *der alte John*, or simply Father Oberholtzer. Thirty years after he became a minister he asked the congregation to elect a younger man to help him with his work. John particularly enjoyed attending the sessions of the General Conference he had helped to create. In 1884 he traveled to Berne, Indiana, for the conference sessions, and three years later, when he was seventy-eight years old, the conference met in his own church. It had grown in size from three congregations in 1860 to thirty-five in 1887.

He did not forget his own East Pennsylvania Conference either. In 1872 it had sent him the following letter of appreciation:

Dear Brother Oberholtzer,

For a long time you have been at the head of our Conference as its leader. Many sad trials it was your lot to encounter. . . . But by the grace of God . . . you have remained calm and firm, and no harm has been permitted to come to you. We, the Eastern Conference, recognize and appreciate the blessings which God has showered upon us through you, and in gratitude we beseech the Lord richly to bless you.

John continued to preach when he was needed, but more often he read the Scripture lesson and led in prayer. Then he would take a chair to one side of the pulpit, usually tilting it back slightly against the wall, and listen to the sermon with his eyes closed. Once the minister stopped in his sermon and said, "Will somebody wake him." He thought John had fallen asleep and might fall off the chair. But John opened his eyes and said, "Oh no, that won't be necessary. I am following the sermon carefully."

On January 13, 1888, three days after his seventy-ninth birthday, he wrote to his old friend Daniel Krehbiel about the leading of God in his life. "Yes. . . we are brothers; brothers in our old age, brothers in confessing our faith in Christ Jesus . . . brothers in our efforts to save the lost, including our own scattered, wandering, and often indifferent and deeply fallen Zion [the Mennonite Church] . . . brothers also in our sometimes lonely prayer room. . . . But I can say to the honor of the Almighty: 'The Lord has done great things for me.' "

One day a few years later he met with the ministers of the East Pennsylvania Conference at the Deep Run Church. At the end of the meeting the chairman asked *Father Oberholtzer* to say a few words. The secretary of the meeting wrote in the minutes: "Our hearts were warmed by his remarks, and began to burn with heavenly fire when upon the announcement of the grand old hymn "Now Thank We All Our God" the aged brother advanced to the organ and led the music without even a note before him."

His last days were spent in the home of his niece, Mrs. William Landis. He remained cheerful and grateful to God for His goodness. One day, while sitting on the couch visiting with a friend, he asked for a glass of water. After drinking it he said, "Now I die." He laid his head on a pillow and had soon gone to be with Jesus, whom he had loved and served long and well.

4

E WILL BE NO SERVICE
AUSE THE MINISTER
CAN'T COME
DAVID TOEWS
WAS HERE

David Toews
1870-1947

David was sixteen years old when he came to Kansas with his parents in the fall of 1886. He loved Kansas. The flat prairie land with its green fields of winter wheat reminded him of the steppes where he had been born in faraway Russia. Thick hedges with fruit that looked like oranges bordered the fields. The meadowlark sang so clearly and carefree that it made him happy, too; and Sand Creek seemed to be whispering softly to him: "Come and fish." He was glad that his parents had chosen Kansas, and especially the town of Newton, to be their new home.

When Sunday came, new friends took David Toews and his family to church with them. The service was in the German language, much like the service had been in Russia. David's father was a minister and so the congregation asked him to tell about their four-year journey to Central Asia and then to Kansas.

"In Russia," David's father began, "there was a man named Klaas Epp. He studied the Bible a great deal, especially the book of Daniel and Revelation. He came to believe that the world would end soon, but that terrible suffering would come to all unfaithful people first. Those who wanted to be saved, Klaas Epp told us, would need to follow him to a special place in Asia where the Lord would prepare a refuge for them. We would be safe there, he said, and the Lord himself would come to us at that place. Because

the Bible does say that the Lord's Day is near, and because we loved the Lord, we and many others believed Klaas Epp."

The congregation noticed that father Toews was deeply moved as he relived these experiences. He continued, "We soon began to sense that Klaas Epp was wrong. We suffered untold hardship. Countless little graves along the road we traveled mark the places where our children were buried because we did not have good food or medical care. Robbers attacked us and finally even murdered some of our young men because they tried to stop them from stealing their sisters as wives. When we finally arrived at our place of refuge, as Klaas Epp called it, the land was very poor, and we had little money to buy seed grain. Then Klaas Epp announced that he was a member of the trinity, like God himself. He would not listen to us at all. There seemed to be no hope." As Father Toews spoke he had a faraway look in his eyes, which told of suffering and despair.

"But," he continued, "God heard our prayers. A letter came from you here in Kansas. You invited us to come here; you offered your help. How we thanked God for such an answer to our prayers. And now," Father Toews concluded, "we are here among you by the grace of God. Thank you for your help. God is faithful."

One morning soon after their arrival

a man in a buggy drawn by two horses drove up to the Toews house. "Good morning," he said to David's father in German. "I am Bernhard Regier. I saw your family in church Sunday and thought your big boy might like a job. I need a good farm hand to help me." David had hoped to go to school, but his father said, "David, you know how badly we need money. You can go to school later. You can learn a great deal from Mr. Regier, even some English. Will you go?"

So David went along with Bernhard Regier. He was sure he would learn English best if he were away from home.

But David was not meant to be a farmer. He worked hard from early morning till late at night caring for the horses, milking the cows, and feeding the pigs, but all the while he kept wishing he could go back to school. He wanted to become a teacher. Sometimes Bernhard Regier wondered whether David was daydreaming, or whether he was just a little bit lonely away from home for the first time. Before many months had passed everyone seemed to agree that David should indeed go to school. In a way he was sorry to leave the Regiers and all the farm animals who were now his friends, but deep down in his heart he was glad to go on to school and leave farming to others.

DAVID BECOMES A TEACHER

"Mother," said David when he came home from school the first day, "I wish I were back on the farm. Everybody is a complete stranger to me, except Johnny whom I met in church. The teacher does everything so differently. I feel I don't know anything at all. Even the little first graders know more than I do; at least they can talk English." David had, in fact, done very little studying

during the four years of travel all over Asia, Europe, and the United States. What if they put him, a big boy of sixteen, into a class with little children? He knew he would die of shame that very day.

But David was a good student. Only the language was hard. "You are too impatient," his father told him. "You will soon speak English very well."

Soon David did indeed understand almost everything that was said, but speaking the strange language was difficult. Once when he tried to answer the teacher, she smiled, and he heard snickering behind him. It made his face hot and his ears tingle. To top it all off, one recess he heard two boys singing behind him:

Dutchman, dutchman, belly full of straw,
Can say nothing but ja, ja, ja!

That was too much for David. Before the two singers knew what had happened, one was rolling on the grass and the other was running for his life with David's swinging fists after him.

Fortunately, the teacher understood how David felt and helped him catch up with his studies. He was a good and cheerful student and a hard worker. He liked to help others, too. Soon he was doing very well in school and had many friends. When he graduated from high school he studied for three years at Halstead Seminary near Newton. And then his dream came true. He was ready to teach.

His first school was in Elbing, a friendly little town just east of Newton. Later he taught in nearby Whitewater and in Newton itself.

One day he received a letter from Gretna, Manitoba. It was from Henry H. Ewert, who had been his teacher in Halstead.

"David," Mr. Ewert wrote, "I need you here. I have been appointed superintendent of schools and am anxious to get as many good teachers into my district as possible. Will you come and join us here? You will love the North."

David had always wanted to see Canada, but he also wanted to attend Bethel College, which had just been founded in Newton. He decided to go to Canada for two years and then return to college. That was in 1893.

The Canadian prairies were fun. In summer the days were so long that he could read without a lamp until ten o'clock at night; in winter the days were very short. He loved the pine forests and wheat fields stretching to the horizon. He loved the deep blue summer sky with its silky white clouds. The cool and gentle breeze made even a warm day seem just right, and in the thundershowers God seemed to scrub the prairies still brighter and cleaner than before. Winter brought its blessings, too. When the snow and the cold came, he loved to sit by a cozy fire and read, or visit with friends about his travels and about things they wanted to do in the years to come. And through it all David became a man—strong as the pine forests in the things he wanted to do, yet gentle as the summer breeze with people who needed help.

David taught school in Manitoba for three years. In his report Superintendent Ewert wrote about him, "He can hardly be recommended too highly," and the secretary of the school district wrote, "He has proved himself a very efficient teacher." Having heard that David was leaving, the secretary added, "I think everybody is sorry he is leaving." Instead of returning to Kansas and Bethel College as he had planned, however, he studied in Winnipeg for two years and then went west to Saskatchewan.

TWO HAPPENINGS

Saskatchewan had not yet become a province of the Dominion of Canada, and so when David came to Rosthern in 1898 he became a true pioneer of the wild West. In that very area the Indians had rebelled against the white man only a few years earlier under Louis Riel's leadership. There were few roads or bridges, few towns or farms—mostly prairie grass and forests. On a cold winter night the howl of the timber wolf and his cousin the coyote sent shivers up David's back, not because he was afraid, but because he felt awe and wonder at the vast empty spaces of the northland. Somehow these howls always made him feel as though he were all alone in the world. Then deep thoughts of life and death, of faith and hope and love would come to his mind until he could fall asleep.

Soon after David's arrival in Rosthern two happenings gave new meaning to his life. He had agreed to teach school in a community called Tiefengrund, located fifteen miles northwest of Rosthern. This new settlement had been established by Mennonite farmers who had just arrived from Germany. And there one day he met Margaret, the blond and blue-eyed daughter of Abram Friesen, a minister. She was nineteen and had been in Canada only five years. She was happy, pretty, and a Christian. It must have been love at first sight. They were married on September 20, 1900, and settled on a homestead which David hoped to farm while he was teaching.

The second happening came about a year later when the congregation called him to be its minister. This was also the year in which their oldest daughter Marie was born. David had a deep personal faith in God. Before he came to Canada he had told the congregation in Kansas of his faith and had been baptized there by his father. Now he was willing to serve as a minister because of his love for Jesus Christ and all the people of God.

David took his work as minister very seriously. One cold and stormy winter day he was to preach at a school five miles away. He walked all the way to the school through the storm because he did not have a team of horses at that time. When he got there he found the following words written on the blackboard: "There will be no service, because the minister can't come." He took a piece of chalk and added four more words: "David Toews was here." Since no one was there for the service, he walked home again. Often he visited his church members on the coldest days of the winter because he knew he would find them at home.

THE RED BRICK HIGH SCHOOL

It was not enough for David to be a good teacher and minister. He had another great dream. "Margaret," he said one day, "we must build a high school and a Bible school to train Christian teachers and other workers to serve in our congregations and on mission fields."

"A good idea," she said, "but where, pray, will you find the money to build the school, and where will you find the teachers?"

"I don't know that yet," he replied, "but things will work out."

And they did. As he prayed and talked to others it became clear that the school should be built in Rosthern, and his friends were convinced that he should be the principal. So the Toews family moved to Rosthern.

Since there was neither money nor time to build a new school, a large old building known as Unruh Hall was rent-ed. A classroom was arranged at one end. Next came the dormitory for students. On the other side of the dormitory was a small apartment for David and Margaret. By now they had three children. Unruh Hall was hot in summer and cold in winter. The furnace smoked so much that the students put up a sign, "Hams smoked here." But during the same year the number of students increased from six to forty-three.

The school just had to move out of smoky, ramshackle Unruh Hall! "How can we have a school without a building?" David would ask everywhere.

Finally some of his friends met with him to talk about what could be done. "We will organize a building committee and plan the building," they said, "if you raise the money."

"But I don't have any money," David replied.

"You know the right people," was their answer.

So David tried. First he traveled to his old home in Kansas, but the people had hardly even heard of Rosthern and showed little interest. Besides, they had their own schools to support. Right there David decided that a school needed to be supported by the people it served, which meant that the money had to be found in Saskatchewan and Alberta. He returned home sad, but wiser.

The people of Saskatchewan were still pioneers. They had food and clothing, but very little money. To collect gifts for the school David drove his horses and buggy from farm to farm asking for donations. Some gave him one dollar, some five, and some much more. Some were selfish and called him "the eternal collector," without giving him anything. Those who had nothing to give often invited him to stay for supper or for the night. One day he came to Henry Bartel's home in Drake, and Mr. Bartel said, "I think I can give $200."

While David was writing the receipt, Mr. Bartel added, "Well, make it $300, and here are $10 dollars for yourself for all your trouble."

He must have known that David often did not get his salary from the school at the end of the month because the other teachers had not yet been paid. There was not enough money for all of them.

Finally the great day came. On the open prairie west of Rosthern, men began digging a basement. Red bricks were hauled in by wagons, and a two-story building slowly came into being. All summer in the year 1910 volunteers worked at the building, and when September came it was ready for the opening of school. On the first floor were two large classrooms. The second floor was made into a dormitory for boys. The furnace was in the basement, and it did not smoke. At first the school was called the German-English Academy, but later its name was changed to Rosthern Junior College. David's dream had come true. His years of sacrifice and patience were well rewarded.

A FRIEND TO ALL IN NEED

The school was very close to David's heart. Sometimes he would say to Margaret, "I wish someone else were principal of this school. Then he could worry about where the money for salaries and supplies should come from, and I could sleep better." But she knew he loved the work in spite of its problems. To work with young people seemed to him the greatest privilege a man could have.

But David was also a minister. There were so many things to do—people to visit, couples to marry, sermons to preach, meetings to attend, and sometimes funerals to take care of. One cold winter day a man came to his office for help. As they visited, David noticed the worn-out shoes of his visitor. Quietly he went to the telephone and called home. "Louise," he said to his daughter, "you know the felt shoes I have in my closet? Bring them to the office right away, will you please?" When she brought them he gave them to the grateful man. Though he was poor himself he was never too poor to share with others in need.

When World War I broke out in 1914 David had even more pastoral work to do. Many young men believed they could not follow Jesus if they joined the army of soldiers being trained to kill the enemy. They believed that Christian love called them to help others rather than to destroy them. But they needed help in understanding the Bible better. Many Christians were saying it was right to go to war. "What does Jesus really want us to do?" they would ask. And so they came to David from far and near because they had heard he understood and could help them. When people called them cowards for not fighting he wrote articles for the papers and explained in public meetings what it means to be a disciple of Jesus Christ. One night a group of men brought a cow into David's church and tied it to the pulpit to show how they hated him and his faith. But he tried to love them, too.

And then deep tragedy struck David and Margaret's home. Early on a cold winter morning in December fire broke out in their home. There were no water hydrants for the fire department to use. Rosthern did not have city water. The house burned to the ground. All escaped to safety, except Irene, the five-year-old sweetheart of the family. By the time they found her she was burned so badly that she died the next day. In trying to rescue her, David himself had almost perished. He was in the hospital when Irene was buried four days later. Yet even now his faith in Christ comforted him, and he was able to say with Job of long ago: "The Lord gave, and the Lord has taken away; blessed be the name of the Lord" (1:21).

CARING FOR TWENTY-THOUSAND REFUGEES

Surely David had enough work to do. He was teacher and minister, chairman of the Canadian conference, and counselor to young men facing the draft. But God acted as He often does. He rewarded David's faithfulness by giving him still greater responsibilities.

A new government had come into power in Russia. The rulers were called Communists because they believed people should share everything they had with all others instead of each one working to own as much as possible for himself. In that way, they believed, everybody would be equal. No one would be rich and no one would be poor. This meant that the Mennonites would also lose their farms. There were over one hundred thousand Mennonites in Russia at that time.

To the Mennonites far more serious than losing their land was the fact that the Communists were atheists. They did not believe in God. Because of this many Mennonites decided to leave Russia as quickly as possible. They sent three men to North America to make arrangements. Soon after their arrival the men found that no refugees from Russia were allowed to come to the United States. So they went to Canada to talk to David Toews.

"Mr. Toews," they said, "you must help us come to Canada. The government in Russia is trying to force everybody to become unbelievers. They have forbidden worship services. They are closing or tearing down our churches. Some of our ministers have been sent to concentration camps in Siberia. We must leave for the sake of communicating our faith to our children. Surely you have enough land here in Canada!"

"Yes," David replied, "we have enough land. You must leave Russia. But where can we find money to buy farms for so many of you? Where can we find money to buy so many travel tickets?" They did not know.

But God knew! He had been getting David Toews ready for just such a time as this. David did not have the money, but he had a faith as big as the universe and a determined will which grew stronger with each new difficulty. When others were discouraged, David always gave them new hope to try again. People trusted him because he was humble and kind and ordinary.

David needed every ounce of courage he had. First he went to Ottawa to receive permission for the refugees to enter Canada. There he soon became the good friend of the Prime Minister of Canada, the Right Honorable William Lyon Mackenzie King, who helped to pass the laws which made it possible for immigrants to come. Next he went to Colonel J. S. Dennis of the Canadian Pacific Railway Company, which people called the CPR, to arrange for transportation. The CPR had ships as well as trains and could bring the Mennonites to Montreal, from where they could take the train.

After they had talked for a while Colonel Dennis asked David, "In which bank do you have the money to pay for all these tickets you want?"

"I have no money," David answered. "We need to borrow every dollar from you, but we will pay it all back with interest."

Colonel Dennis was quiet for a long time. He looked into the tired face of the man before him and knew he could not say no. He had never met a calmer, more determined man. He had never seen eyes more filled with hope. And so at length he said, "I know the Mennonites, and trust them. I trust you, too, David Toews. You can have all the money you need for the refugees."

Did David really know what he was doing? By the time the last refugee was to come to Canada the total amount borrowed would be two million dollars with interest. People were to say he had no right to promise they would pay that much. Some would even accuse him of keeping money for himself. Twenty-five years were to pass before it would all be paid back. No, David did not know how everything would end. He simply did what needed to be done—the refugees had to be rescued. For the rest he trusted God. Often when walking home from the office late at night, or while traveling to some farm home on his wagon, he would softly sing a song that had become dear to him. In the German it was known as *Befiehl du deine Wege*:

Commit your every journey,
Your sorrow and your fear,
To him who rules the heavens,
Whose strength is always near;
He who does guide the tempest,
And shows the clouds their way,
Will surely find a good path,
On which my feet can stay.

And even if the devil,
Should threaten and destroy,
Still God in his great mercy,
Will grant us victory;
For what he has determined,
To be his will for men,

Will surely come to pass,
In his appointed time.

Translated by C. J. Dyck

And then the great day came. At five o'clock on the afternoon of July 21, 1923, a long train with ten passenger and three baggage cars pulled into the Rosthern station with the first group of seven hundred immigrants. They were very happy to be there. Many of them cried. As they stood on the station platform of their new home they thought of the wonderful leading of God and softly they began to sing:

Now thank we all our God,
With heart and hands and
voices,
Who wondrous things hath done . . .

Those who had come to meet them joined in the song until it echoed across the prairie from a thousand voices. The bystanders had never heard such singing. One of them said to David, "Is that the kind of immigrants you are bringing in? Why, then bring in lots of them."

Many more were indeed to come. In all they numbered 20,201 when every child had been counted. How David and his helpers worked to find farms for them! Some did not want to farm and needed jobs. A few were sorry they had come and blamed David for all their troubles. Some of the old-time Mennonites in Canada worked against David because they did not want to help pay the debts he had made with the CPR to help the Mennonites from Russia. Most of the immigrants, however, were happy in their new home. They called David the "Moses of the Mennonites," because he had helped them to leave Russia and come to Canada like Moses

had led the children of Israel out of Egypt into the promised land.

NONE OF US LIVES FOR HIMSELF ONLY

The years had gone by so quickly that David hardly realized he was growing old. His hair had become snow white. He walked slowly and with a cane. He became hard-of-hearing. One day blond and blue-eyed Margaret, who had grown old with him, died and was buried in the cemetery in Rosthern. Now he was lonely even though he had many friends. But he knew he would soon join her. Because he had been so active all his life it was hard for David to sit back and let others do the work.

He made one more trip to Kansas. His work had kept him from ever going back to enroll as a student at Bethel College, but now the college wanted to confer on him an honorary Doctor of Divinity degree because of his many years of faithful service in the name of Christ.

A beautiful statement describing his work was read before he received the degree. It began with the words, "We present a man with an enviable record of achievement in ministering to fundamental needs of humanity, a pioneer of the North." It cheered his heart to know that his work was deeply appreciated even by people far away in Kansas.

But David still had one big problem —the debt to the CPR had to be repaid. He had given his word of honor as a Christian, in the name of the Mennonite Church; this word must not be broken. Not to pay a debt seemed to David to be like stealing someone else's money. Now he was too old to do any more work on it, but others carried on. Would they succeed in paying it off, or would he die feeling he had taken other people's money and not paid it back?

The time which people called "The Depression" were years of crop failures. Instead of rain and sunshine, almost every day had brought a new prairie sand-storm. Thistles grew everywhere and the wind blew them up against the fences until posts and wire were completely covered by them and the drifting sand. It was very hard for the immigrant farmers to pay back their travel debt. Most of them sent their teen-age and older daughters to the cities, not to go to college, but to work as housemaids for five dollars a month to help pay back the borrowed money. Some of the immigrants had enough money, but instead of using it to pay their share they used it to buy cars or furniture or more land.

In spite of all this, however, the debt grew smaller and smaller because most of the immigrants and their friends believed that a Christian must always pay his debts. One day Jacob Thiessen, the man who carried on David's work of collecting money to repay the debt, came to him and said, "The debt is paid!"

"What did you say?" David asked.

Jacob Thiessen put his mouth close to David's almost deaf ear and said again loudly, "The debt is paid in full."

But David could not believe it. "You are just saying that to make me feel good before I die," he said.

But Jacob shook his head gently and said again, "The debt is paid!"

Then David believed it. He became very quiet. A few big tears rolled down his wrinkled cheek as the burden of the two million dollar debt was lifted from his life.

"Jacob," he said softly, "God has heard our prayers. Now I can die in peace."

Three months later, on February 25, 1947, he died at his home in Rosthern. At his funeral Jacob Thiessen preached on the text, "Do you not know that a prince and a great man has fallen this day in Israel?" (2 Sam. 3:38). He had indeed been a prince or king in his faith and courage. He had loved God and his fellowmen.

Ten years later the Rosthern Junior College built a large, beautiful new building to replace the old red brick schoolhouse. On the cornerstone the builders engraved these words: "In memory of David Toews, erected September 29, 1957." Society also set a memorial to him. In 1964 the government of the Province of Saskatchewan named a lake "Toews Lake" after him. In its memorial it said:

> Saskatchewan's finest resource is the character and quality of her peoples: It is appropriate that her geographical features perpetuate the names and honour the work of those prominent in development of the Province, and those who gave dedicated service to fellow citizens.

> Toews Lake is named after Bishop David Toews. Latitude: 57° 17' Longitude 105° 00'. Certified by the Canadian Permanent Committee on Geographical Names. Signed: Minister of Natural Resources.

The words of the Apostle Paul in Romans 14:7 also summed up his life of faith: "None of us lives for himself only, none of us dies for himself only; if we live, it is for the Lord that we live, and if we die, it is for the Lord that we die. Whether we live or die, then, we belong to the Lord." That had always been one of David's favorite Bible verses.

5

Cornelius (C.F.) Klassen 1894-1954

God is love. 1 John 4:8

Carefully Cornelius went over the contents of his big brown leather suitcase for the last time. It was all there—the new suit which the village tailor had finished sewing just in time, new shoes from his father's store, and the long white shirt with stand-up collar and wide black leather belt. There was his pencil box and writing pad, his Bible, handkerchiefs his mother had made, the new jackknife, and in one corner the most important item of them all, a new razor and shaving soap. He was certain he would need these before he returned home, for he was already twelve years old and practically a man.

"Cornelius," his father called, "are you ready? It's almost time to go. We don't want you to miss the train."

"Coming," he answered, as he took one last look around the room.

He picked up his suitcase and carried it to the wagon. It was heavier than he thought it would be. Then he said good-bye to his brothers and his sister. It was hard to say good-bye to his mother. She was always so good to him. He felt like crying. And then they were off. His brother Henry had begged to go along, and sat beside him.

The thirty-one miles to the station went by much too quickly. No one talked a great deal, but each knew what the other was thinking. Cornelius was leaving home for the first time, to study at the Mennonite school in Karassan, in the

Crimea region of southern Russia. Life would be very different for him and for those at home without him.

Suddenly his father said, "Cornelius, there is something about which I want to talk to you."

In the silent moments that followed, Cornelius knew that it would be something important. Most likely it would be a reminder not to forget daily Bible reading and prayer. Perhaps he would talk about the need of going to church regularly. But when his father spoke, it was about none of these, as if he took them for granted.

What he did say was, "Cornelius, you know that you carry my name. Whatever you do, whether good or bad, no matter where you are, will also reflect on me your father."

Cornelius had never thought of it in that way. He felt very close to his father. How his father must trust him! He resolved right there never to do anything that might spoil the good name of his father, which was now also his own.

School Away from Home

Life was indeed different at home without Cornelius. At first Henry thought he could not get along without his older brother. He hid in the barn and cried when they returned from taking Cornelius to the train because he believed he would never see him again. And he did not see him for three years. The high school was seven hundred miles away, travel was very expensive, and summer vacations were short. But how Henry enjoyed every letter Cornelius wrote, telling about his studies and friends and experiences.

The day came when Cornelius graduated, with honors, and returned home.

"Why, Cornelius," his mother said when she saw him, "I hardly know you. You have grown so tall and handsome."

And he hardly knew his own family anymore because they had grown also. Little John and Nick had been born while he was gone. There were now ten children—Cornelius, the oldest, was just sixteen; then Frank, Gerhard, Peter, Henry, Abraham, Jacob, sister Justina, and of course the two baby boys.

"Are you going away to school again?" Henry asked his oldest brother one day soon after he returned, "or are you staying home with us now?"

"Yes," he answered, "I am going away to school again. I want to study medicine to become a medical doctor. But first, I want to stay right here for a whole year to get to know you all again and to help father in the store." That is what he did.

During this year a deep change came over Cornelius' inner spirit. As he dusted shelves in the store and unpacked shipments of fresh supplies, he often thought about his own life and about God. He could not remember a time when he had not known about Jesus, but now he felt a particular need of Him. His life and death and love took on a new and deeper meaning than ever before, until he decided to give himself completely into His care forever and to do what Jesus would tell him to do. Writing about this much later, his brother Henry said, "He never did anything halfheartedly. So this dedication, too, was with his whole heart; it determined the course

of his entire life and work." He was baptized and became a member of the Mennonite Brethren congregation at New Samara where he lived.

Before the family had quite realized it the year was gone, and once again Cornelius packed his suitcase to go to school. This time he went to Moscow, the huge capital city of Russia.

Soon he wrote back, "I have found a job with the Otto Deutz Company. If I work part-time I can pay my bills and study at the same time, while my studies go begging." Another letter came, from a different address, which said, "I am in St. Petersburg now, and have found an excellent teacher to help me prepare for medical school."

Then came World War I. He sensed that a great storm which would change the course of history was gathering over mankind, but he could not see into the future. He was glad to leave that in the hands of God. Meanwhile, the government ordered him to work in the forests of Russia, planting trees and fighting fires with other young men, because he refused to join the army as a soldier. His faith grew strong in the quiet beauty of the wilderness. In his own way God was preparing him even then for great service to mankind.

BREAD, BREAD! IN GOD'S NAME, BREAD!

"I tell you," said Cornelius to his friend Peter Froese, "this government cannot last much longer. It ignores the needs of millions of poor peasants and favors the rich."

"If the peasants ever rebel," Peter replied, "it will be rough indeed; I'd rather not be around then."

And rebel they did. On March 12, 1917, the Czar abdicated his throne because of the revolution. In a second revolution eight months later the Bolsheviks took control of the government of Russia.

There was actually very little government of any kind for several years. All did as they pleased. The new government could do little to stop them. The situation spelled anarchy. Thousands of people were killed by robbers or their own neighbors who wanted their property. Nestor Machno was a particularly cruel bandit. In the county of Zagradovka he and his followers killed 240 Mennonite men, women, and children in November of 1919. Compared with the poor peasants most Mennonites were rich. The peasants wanted their farms and their money.

All over Russia people hid in fear. Farms and dairies and gardens were neglected. The good wheat which farmers had kept for seed was stolen or confiscated by the government. The poor wheat which they had left to plant did not grow well. Rain failed to come in time for the wheat to grow. The grass dried up and cattle starved. Soon many parts of Russia were practically without food. People could not even buy bread or potatoes or meat. All the food was gone. Many went begging from door to door, crying "Bread! BREAD! In God's name, bread!" But there was none. People ate mice, crows, cats, dogs, and even the bark of trees in the forests to stay alive. And many—several million of them—starved to death. It seemed as if a curse hung over the entire land.

And where was Cornelius? Did he survive? Indeed he did.

"Peter," he said to his friend one day, "we must do something to help our farmer friends in the villages."

"Yes, we must," Peter replied, "but what?"

They soon had an idea. Together with others they founded an agricultural soci-ety to help farmers with seed wheat, machinery, and horses. But the government thought they were opposing the progress of the revolution and put them all into the terrible Lubjanka prison in Moscow. Cornelius was put into solitary confinement like a dangerous criminal. But God had other plans, and after a time they were released.

Meanwhile, they heard that four of their friends had been sent to America to get help and that the American Mennonites were sending flour, meat, and clothing. Some of it had already arrived in the needy villages. One day Peter received a secret message that an American was looking for him. Could he come to the Savoy Hotel? He went immediately, wondering who this could be. Soon he spotted a man in the lobby of the hotel who seemed to be waiting for someone. He went to him and said in German, "I am Peter Froese. Are you looking for me?"

"Oh, yes," the American answered, "I am Alvin J. Miller. The Mennonites of America are sending food to help you. I am their representative."

How surprised Cornelius was when Alvin J. Miller was introduced to him. They talked and planned long into the night. It was decided that Cornelius would take him on a quick tour of the famine areas to see where they might best help. In his next letter to the United States Alvin J. Miller wrote about his meeting with the two men. "Cornelius Klassen," he wrote, "is a man of distinguished appearance. Both Klassen and Froese are young in years, but old, indeed aged, in experience."

Cornelius never forgot that trip with Alvin J. Miller. Wherever they went people were hungry and dying for want of food. But in the villages where the American flour and meat had arrived, there was great joy. "Let me describe only one of my experiences," he said later at a meeting. "I came to a family with very many children. The faces and legs of mother and father were swollen from hunger. The children were only skin and bones. The mother mixed some of the fresh flour to make biscuits, while the older daughter tried to light a fire in the stove. It had not been used for a long time and smoked badly, but at last the wood began to burn. First the mother put some of the fat from the American supplies into the frying pan. Then she picked up the biscuit batter as though it were holy bread, and cooked the first biscuits. The children all stood around the stove. The mother could not restrain herself any longer and cried softly. Her tears rolled down her swollen cheeks and dripped onto the stove. But the eyes of the children! I shall never forget them. I could not control my feelings any longer, and quietly slipped out of the house."

The following winter was cold and hard. There were not enough relief supplies for everyone. Horses and men were so weak that they could hardly haul the supplies from the railroad station through the deep snow to the villages. Often robbers killed the drivers and took the food because they were hungry, too. But finally spring came. The cattle and horses had fresh grass to eat. Gardens grew. The rains came in time for the wheat. The famine of 1921-22 was over.

But for Cornelius famine relief was only the beginning of his work for others. He had fallen in love with pretty Mary Brieger and married her, but there was no time for a honeymoon. Many Mennonites had decided to leave Russia. They wanted to live in freedom without fear and longed to worship God as they believed the Bible taught. They knew they could do this in Canada, if only they could get there. Cornelius worked with many others to help them leave, often at the risk of his own life because the government did not want them to leave.

One day in 1924 his father died. Soon after the funeral Cornelius said to his mother, "Mother, you and the children must go to Canada, too. I will arrange your passports and everything for you." She agreed. A year later everything was ready and he accompanied them to London, but planned to return to Moscow.

"Please, come with us," his mother and brothers and sisters begged. "Mary and the boys can follow later."

"No," he replied, "my people need me yet; I will come when I can."

With the help of many others besides Cornelius over twenty thousand persons emigrated to Canada, and just before no more were allowed to leave, Cornelius and Mary, together with Harold and Walfried, were able to leave also. It was Christmas, 1928, when they arrived in snowy and peaceful Winnipeg. How grateful they were to be alive and free! God had indeed answered their prayers.

A NEW HOME IN CANADA

"Mary," Cornelius said to his wife soon after they arrived, "we must learn English. It feels awful not to know what people are talking about. Why, I can't even read the newspaper."

"Yes," she said, "that's true, but our children will probably learn it faster than we will."

That was also true. But the parents learned it too, although Cornelius did so more quickly than Mary because he traveled a great deal. The church had asked him to visit the new immigrants, to help and encourage them and to tell them what he knew about their relatives in Russia.

On one of these trips he stopped in Rosthern, Saskatchewan, to visit his new friend David Toews who had done so much to make the migration to Canada possible.

"Cornelius," David said after several cups of coffee and a piece of rhubarb cake, "we need you for a very difficult work. You know we borrowed most of the money to bring all these immigrants to Canada. Their travel tickets cost us almost two million dollars. We need you to encourage the immigrants to pay it back; we need you to collect the money."

"Not me," he replied. "Let someone else do that. I want to live a normal life for a change."

"But you know the people better than anyone else," David replied. "They respect you for having helped them to come here. You are the man."

"Let me think and pray about it," Cornelius said. "I will write you my answer."

Not long after the meeting the answer came that if God wanted him to do it, as he believed He did, then he would accept the assignment.

For the next fifteen years Cornelius traveled from one end of Canada to the other, from British Columbia to Ontario, and even to the Maritime Provinces and the settlements in the far north. He visited the immigrants, he encouraged them, and collected the payment for their tickets to Canada. Some tried to forget the debt. Some accused Cornelius of keeping the money for himself. Once a woman shouted at him, "If you don't get out of my house right away I will pour this pot of boiling water over you." He decided to come back later. But the day came when the last debt was paid and David Toews, who had signed for the loan, could die in peace.

HUMILITY

Could Cornelius settle down now to a normal life at home with his family? Hardly. Another war, World War II, had broken out in Europe, and Canadian young men were drafted into the army to help England. Those who refused to become soldiers had to appear before a judge for a hearing and then do alternative work in forests and hospitals. Cornelius was often asked to help these young men if they appeared before a certain judge in Winnipeg who considered them all yellow cowards. The judge could be so mean that Cornelius, even though outwardly he remained calm and courteous, became very angry deep inside.

One Sunday morning, while Cornelius was in church, his mind wandered to the judge again. With a start he suddenly said to himself, "I hate that judge! That is sin. This hatred is destroying my spiritual life. I must do something about it."

He ate a quiet Sunday dinner and then he said, "Mary, I am going to see the judge. I must ask his forgiveness." And he drove off.

The judge himself answered the doorbell. When he saw Cornelius he assumed that he wanted to see him about one of the hearings for the boys, but Cornelius said, "Judge, may I speak to you personally?"

"Why, yes," said the judge, "come on in."

Cornelius said, "Judge, I have come to ask your forgiveness. I found out in church this morning that I hated you deep inside, and that is sin. I asked Jesus to forgive me, and I want to ask you, too. Christ taught us to love, not to hate our fellowmen."

"But, Mr. Klassen," said the judge, "you have always been a perfect gentleman to me. I don't know what you're talking about."

"Nevertheless," said Cornelius, "deep inside I hated you, and that is wrong. Will you forgive me?"

"Why, yes, I surely will," said the judge with deep feeling.

"Thank you," said Cornelius, "and may God give you strength for your heavy responsibilities as judge of the King's bench."

More Refugees

Cornelius could hardly wait for the war to end. He wanted to get back into Russia to help the Mennonites who were still there. Soon reports came to him of thousands of refugees who had fled before the fighting armies and were scattered all over the bombed-out cities of Germany. In 1945 the Mennonite Central Committee (MCC) sent him to find them. Would he be able to help them? Were any left alive? His friends feared that the Russian army might arrest him and take him back to Russia for having helped so many Mennonites escape after the first World War. He feared that, too, but went anyway.

On the first trip Cornelius spent eighteen weeks looking for refugees. Though they hid out of fear of the armies, he found many of them. One day as he was searching for possible refugees in the rubble of a devastated city he heard soft music. As he came closer he heard voices singing the familiar German song, *"Ist's auch eine Freude, Mensch geboren sein . . . ."* He had found another group. He seemed like an angel of heaven to them.

Soon he spent most of his time with the refugees in Europe. A huge camp was set up for them at Gronau on the Dutch-German border. Here they were safe and cared for. In addition, they were given medical checkups, passports, and tickets to go on to Canada. Those who failed to pass Canadian immigration regula-tions were comforted and helped to try again later, or to emigrate to Paraguay and Uruguay in South America. Cornelius knew most of them by name—eventually nearly fifteen thousand persons—and he knew most of their relatives in Canada, too. He rarely forgot a name he heard once or the face of a person he met.

And he never gave up hope. When everything seemed hopeless he would say quietly, "God is able," or "It will be interesting to see how the Lord works it out this time."

One day there seemed to be no more hope that a family whose members were in poor health could go to Canada. As Cornelius talked with the Canadian officials they said, "Mr. Klassen, we are very sorry, but the case is closed."

"No," he responded, "it is not closed."

"It isn't?" they asked surprised. "What do you mean?"

"I mean," he said, "that the Lord has not spoken yet. The case is not closed."

Cornelius was so full of hope because he prayed much. God was very real to him. An MCC worker who did not know him once asked to drive along with him from Gronau to southern Germany. "I was terribly afraid," she reported later, "because he drove so fast. But then it was time for breakfast. Before we ate, Brother Klassen prayed. I will never forget that prayer." His humility and complete dependence upon God so strengthened her, she said, "It didn't matter after that how fast he drove. I knew we would be safe." His friends still thought he drove too fast.

One night he was driving on the German *autobahn*. His thermos bottle with coffee fell over on the floor. As he bent down to pick it up, he slammed into the back of a semi-trailer without lights. The car was a wreck, but Cornelius was not seriously hurt. "What would become of

us if you were no longer here to help us?" the refugees said to him when they heard of his narrow escape. "Please get a chauffeur to drive for you so you can rest."

But he replied simply, "God will take care of me."

Those who went on trips with him soon discovered that he always started out at five in the morning, regardless of how late the meeting had been the night before. Then at sunrise he would pull over to the side of the road and stop to pray. But they also discovered that after Cornelius had said, "God is able," he told himself, "and now get to work and do your part." Whenever friends visited him he would not let them leave without having prayer with them. He called it kneeling fellowship. Everything he did seemed to point to the power of God rather than to what he himself could do.

Cornelius was often lonely. He had sacrificed not only his own life but also a part of his family life for the sake of Christ. Once he wrote, "I am often very lonely. Especially when I am traveling, the separation from my family becomes almost unbearable." The war had broken up many families. Among the refugees there was often a son or daughter missing, a mother or father gone. Gradually it became one of his greatest longings to unite as many of these families as possible, and for this goal he sacrificed the blessings of being with his own family. One day, not long before he died, he said, "I have been able to bring one more family together." This made him very happy.

AND THEN HE DIED

A serious heart problem bothered Cornelius again one evening as he drove to Gronau, the refugee center he knew and loved. Upon his arrival he was hospitalized at once, but after the doctor had gone, Cornelius said to the nurse, "I am leaving tomorrow morning for a conference in Holland."

His car was still there at five the next morning, however. A few hours later he left on a much greater journey; he went to be with Jesus, whom he loved and served. Mary and the children and many friends gently laid him to rest in a grave in Frankfurt, Germany — far from his old home in Russia and far from his new home in British Columbia. But it did not matter. They knew his real home was with God.

Many memorial services were held for him later, particularly in Canada where most Mennonites knew him. High tributes were given to his life and work. His life had been given to the refugees, but he had done much more. Men spoke of his help in starting a college in Winnipeg and a Bible School in Switzerland. He had helped found a newspaper for refugees. He had helped establish three homes for old people in Germany. He had been a member of many, many committees, especially under MCC. One man called him the Secretary of State of the Mennonites; another identified him as a "hero —a Mennonite who incorporated faith and action, love and service."

But the greatest thing that could be said of him was that he was a man of God. He was a man of simple faith, deep love, and never-ending hope.

6

Nicolai Siemens
1895-1953

Behold, the Lord's hand is not shortened, that it cannot save. Isaiah 59:1

"Well, here he is, our darling, and our hearts are happy for him. There were many difficulties to be overcome, to be sure, before he could see the light of day, but these now make him even more welcome. . . . He is poorly dressed, as you can see, but that is how it is for children of pioneers. Some of you will be surprised and ask, 'But why doesn't he wear a cap?' Listen, dear reader, this is why: We do not have the capital letters yet to print a large heading. Besides, this baby will not be given a name until the next meeting of the Colony administration. . . ."

The man who wrote these words was Nicolai Siemens. The time was October, 1930. The place was Paraguay in South America where a starry Southern Cross shines in the sky at night instead of the Big Dipper. He was describing his small new newspaper, which he had printed on a hand-operated press brought to Paraguay from Russia. He loved that little paper almost as much as he loved his own ten children. It had only four pages, and for a time he had thought it would never get started. The press was broken, there was no money to repair it, and no place to set it up. But finally he could start printing, and the words just quoted appeared on the first page of the first issue. By the time the second issue appeared, the paper had a name. It was called *Menno Blatt,* which means "a newspaper for Mennonites."

Nicolai Siemens, together with many other refugees, had come to Paraguay from Russia in 1930. Many of the immigrants were very disappointed in their new homeland. It was hot and dry and far from civilization. But where they saw only a cactus, Nicolai saw a beautiful flower; and where they saw bad luck, he saw the hand of God. He was a teacher. But he also wanted to publish a paper to encourage the settlers in their pioneering, to help them with problems, and to make them feel closer to each other. He wanted the paper to keep them from forgetting God.

Years later, whenever I, the author, visited the Fernheim (meaning "far from home") Colony in Paraguay, Siemens would bring me a copy of the last edition of the *Menno Blatt,* and say, "I thought you might enjoy the morning paper." We both knew, of course, that it only came out once a month, but that was not important. And then he and I and others would sit down and talk. He was a great storyteller. And we would listen and ask questions as he told of Russia, of the early years of pioneering, and of his hope for the future. He was full of hope. He trusted God in everything.

This, in his own words as told to the author and as he described it in his twenty-five years of editing the *Menno Blatt, i*s the story of his life and that of the pioneers in Paraguay.

Moscow 1929

The first thing I remember about my childhood is that my parents left Russia for America when I was three years old. It was a long journey. I know I wanted to stand at the railing and watch the big waves, but for some reason my parents wouldn't let me. They settled at Bingham Lake, Minnesota, where they had relatives. But they didn't like it in the United States, and three years later when I was six years old, they packed up again and went back to Russia.

I enjoyed school very much, especially reading and reciting poetry. Mathematics was not very interesting. Our classes were all in German, but we also studied Russian, which I enjoyed. No, I don't remember getting into trouble at school, except that the teacher often told me to stop daydreaming and get to work. When I was fifteen I was baptized and joined the Mennonite Brethren Church. Soon after, I was asked to help teach a Sunday school class, and when I was twenty-one I was elected a minister in the church. I knew I wanted to be a teacher, but being a minister was not a full-time job then. We had many ministers who shared in the work and all earned their living doing something else. It seemed wrong to our people then to be paid for doing church work.

I married Margarethe Janzen and we were very happy. But two years later, soon after our little Grete was born, Margarethe died. I don't know why God let it happen, but I know He has a plan for every life, and I trust Him. I was lonely with only Grete, and she needed a mother. So after a year I married Anna Wosnjak. We had eight more daughters and two sons. One daughter died in a refugee camp in Germany.

Soon after my second marriage I went to Dschangraw Bible School for two years, and when it was closed, I studied one more year at Orenburg. Then we returned to my home village of Smolja-nowka in Siberia, where I served as minister. But this was hard. Because the government officials did not believe in God, we were forbidden to teach religion to our children in school. Many schools were closed, too, and we were suspected of being traitors. Many of our people had beautiful farms, which made their neighbors jealous. Because of this, many Mennonites emigrated to Canada.

By 1929 things were so bad that most of the Mennonites wanted to leave Russia. Soon over twenty thousand of us were in Moscow trying to leave. The government said we could not go. Every night trainloads of our people were shipped back into Russia in freight cars. It often happened that families became separated. Some of our people died. And we prayed as we waited for our turn to be shipped back.

Then one day a miracle happened. Officers came to us and said we could leave Russia, the sooner the better. We could hardly believe our ears, but it was true. Soon five thousand five hundred of us were in refugee camps in Germany and then no more were allowed to leave. We thanked God for our freedom and prayed for those who could not come. We thought we would all go to Canada immediately. About two thousand of our people did. But Canada would take no more refugees because of the depression. There were already too many people without work. Now we had nowhere to go. Germany could not keep us either. Surely God had brought us out of Russia for a purpose.

God answered our prayers this time through the Mennonite Central Committee (MCC) of North America. The Mennonites there had helped us during the famine in Russia, and now they offered to pay for our travel to Paraguay and to help us get settled. "Paraguay," we said. "Where is that?" We began to read about it in encyclopedias. What we read did not encourage us. It said that Paraguay was hot and wild. But we were told that some Mennonites from Canada had already settled there and were doing well. Finally many of us were ready to go. We took it as the will of God for us. Some decided to go to Brazil instead, which MCC did not like because there the immigrants would not be free from military service. Fortunately the Mennonites in Holland were able to help them.

We sailed for Paraguay in fear and in hope. Would we be able to live there in freedom and have enough to eat? We had wanted to go to Canada where most of us had relatives. Their letters had assured us that it was a good land. "But Paraguay," we said. "What will it be like?"

THE CHACO

After traveling more than a month we arrived in Asuncion, the capital of Paraguay, on April 16, 1930. The President of Paraguay, Dr. Jose P. Guggiari, welcomed us and took some of us to see the city. Before evening, however, we continued up river to the Chaco, which was to be our home.

We stopped at many river ports on the way. It seemed strange to see women carrying huge baskets on their heads. The baskets were filled with fruit or vegetables, or even live chickens with their legs tied together. We couldn't understand a word the people said.

How we wished that we could settle by the river! But instead, we traveled ninety miles inland on a small railroad. There we were met by the settlers who had gone there earlier from Canada and who took us another seventy-five miles inland by ox cart. My, my, those oxen! Have you ever ridden an ox cart? Their normal speed is two miles an hour; three is definitely high gear. And they stir up so much dust with their dragging hoofs! One morning they were all gone. It took almost till noon to find them in the bush. We had to delay our start until mid-afternoon when everybody had had his *siesta,* which lasted several hours. It is too hot to travel at noon. Those oxen are so lazy and stubborn! Sometimes they just lie down on the road and refuse to go. I have known men who finally lit a little fire under them to get them up. On the other hand, once they make up their mind to go in a certain direction you can't stop them either. Driving oxen is a good test of patience and Christian character. And, after all, those who drive with oxen and those who save much time by driving cars all celebrate New Year's Day on the same day. So why hurry?

ALONE IN THE WILDERNESS

When we finally arrived at the site for our homes, the drivers unloaded our baggage and left. Now we were all alone in the wilderness. Except for snakes! We had been warned about snakes. But soon we found that they left us alone, if we left them alone. One night a snake crawled into the pajama sleeve of one of the women while she was sleeping and bit her when she tried to pull her arm out, but she did not get sick. Soon we became careless and walked barefooted everywhere. Then accidents happened. Paul Schroeder, a four-year-old boy, stuck his hand into an old pile of trees and was bitten. He died the next day. We had no medicine to help him. Another boy, John Unruh, who was thirteen, was bitten in the foot, but he lived. He was sick for four months, however.

While we were still in the refugee camps in Germany, we had divided the whole group into villages of twenty-five families each. Now we immediately chose locations for these villages and pitched our tents. The tents were very hot. We knew we had to do two things quickly— build mud houses which would be cooler, and dig wells. One well had been dug for us, but it was three miles away and threatened to run dry. Water trickled into it so slowly, and we needed it so badly that we often had a boy sitting at the well with a cup to catch the water and pour it into a bucket as soon as a little had collected.

Digging wells was dangerous and discouraging. Many wells produced only salt water, which we could not drink. Several children died because it was the only water they had. The village of Au-hagan dug nine wells and they were all salty. The settlers gave up. Later they dug another one and it had sweet water. Digging wells was dangerous because the soil was sandy and could easily cave in, burying the digger below. We had no boards to make cribbing inside the hole to prevent cave-ins. In the village of Schoenwiese Henry Cornelsen had dug down twenty-five feet when the well caved in and buried him. There were others. Still, we had to dig wells if we were to survive.

Building houses was easier. We would dig a big hole about five feet square and one foot deep. Into that we shoveled dirt, added water and grass, and then tramped everything thoroughly with our bare feet. Then we put the mixture into a box about one foot long and five inches thick, and dumped it onto the ground to dry in the sun. That was our brick. If it rained while the bricks were drying, they all dissolved and we had to start over. The roof was made of branches covered with long grass mixed with mud. Later we brushed the floor and inside walls with cow manure to give them a smooth, hard finish. We left holes in the walls for windows and hung sacks over them. Later we had shutters. It was many years until we had glass.

TYPHUS

Soon after we arrived a terrible epidemic of typhus struck us. At first we did not know what it was. People were dying everywhere, but we thought this happened because of the heat and poor food. We had no doctor. Finally when a doctor was sent to us, we knew. He innoculated us and after three weeks the epidemic was over. Ninety-four persons had died. It was a terrible time. People still refer to it as *das grosse Sterben* (the great death). Almost everybody was sick, but wells had to be dug and fields cleared and planted. We had no boards for coffins, so we cut down the big bottle trees and hollowed them out. Soon we had to hunt far and wide for more trees. People were so weak they could hardly dig graves for their friends. Water was scarce, and the tents were extremely hot, especially for those who lay in them with a high fever. I remember a tent in which everybody had died. The dolls lay on the floor, but there was no one to play with them. Then we really learned to pray. In the *Menno Blatt* I printed the text: "Behold, the Lord's hand is not shortened, that it cannot save" (Is. 59: 1). He heard our prayers. The plague ended.

A THANKSGIVING SERVICE

But we were not discouraged. Some doubted that God had had anything to do with bringing us here, but many of us knew that He had. Our crops were beginning to grow. Already we were eating some of our home-grown food. We had a school for our children, but not a building, so the children studied outdoors. Sometimes wild oxen came and the children had to hide behind trees. We held church services outdoors also. We even had a baptismal service the first year. It is our custom to immerse people to baptize them, but we had no lake or river nearby. So we dug a pit and after a heavy rain had filled it we had the baptismal service.

One of the most important events in the colony was a thanksgiving service on November 25, a year after we had received permission to leave Moscow. Some might think it foolish; we were poor, very busy, and sometimes discouraged. We had just experienced the terrible typhus epidemic. But we wanted to thank God for His deliverance, and we wanted to thank our brothers around the world for helping us. As a part of the service we drew up a statement of thanksgiving to all who had helped us and signed it. It is printed in the December, 1930, issue of *Menno Blatt*. We have had a similar service of thanksgiving every year since, always on November 25. A commonly used Bible text is the one we used the first time: "Offer to God a sacrifice of thanksgiving, and pay your vows to the Most High; and call upon me in the day of trouble; I will deliver you, and you shall glorify me" (Ps. 50:14, 15).

We have so much to be thankful for. People complain about the heat. It does go up to 115, even 120 degrees in the shade, but it gets hot in Texas, too. Take our spring, for example. Once you have experienced it you will never forget it. Our late winter days are very hot, and we often have miserable sandstorms. For days, and sometimes weeks, north winds blow sand into every crack. Our eyes begin to hurt. It is almost impossible to work, but we must. We do not even feel like eating—only drinking. It is hard to sleep at night, and even if we do, we wake up tired in the morning.

But then comes spring. A fog suddenly seems to gather in the north. Grandfather complains about his rheumatism. The salt in the salt bowl on the table grows damp. The chalk writes clearer on the blackboard at school. A woman tells her neighbor that she saw her dog eating grass, and the neighbor reports that the new moon tips pointed straight down last night. "Yes," they agree, "the weather is about to change." They are right.

Soon dark clouds appear on the horizon in the south, and tumbling over each other, fill the sky. In the space of a few seconds the wind shifts from the north to due south. Lightning flashes, and thunder roars louder than we ever heard it in Russia. And then the rain comes. We can smell it as it closes in. First a few drops fall, then more and more, and finally there are great sheets of water, so all we see is water everywhere. The rain ends as quickly as it came, but the cool breeze continues.

That is only the beginning, however. A strange noise is heard coming from the ponds and ditches. It can be frightening to those who have never heard it. It is a frog concert! Some frogs are as big as a cap. Others are very small. All join in the orchestra. I have sometimes wished I could record that symphony and take it to Europe for frog concerts. Soon crickets join the chorus, and then birds without number, dressed in all the colors of the rainbow, start singing. A wild sow leads her litter to a mudhole, and a deer leaps by with a fawn. And when night comes, millions of little fireflies illuminate the miracle of life around us. Spring in the Chaco is a truly marvelous experience.

There is a mystery about fish that we cannot solve. Soon after a heavy rain we notice little fish in what used to be dry holes. How do they get there? Do they lie in the dry ground like the frogs, waiting for the rain? One man here thinks ducks carry fish eggs on their feathers and legs from the river to these small lakes.

A topic of much greater importance in our colony, however, is the rain itself. Do you think we can cause rain by praying for it? Soon after we arrived we began to experience long periods of drouth. Sometimes it became so dry that our cattle died because there was no grass to eat. Then people began to call for prayer meetings. Surely God could help if we asked Him. "His hand is not shortened that it cannot save," we said. But some argued that prayer could not change the climate of the Chaco which has been like this since time began. Others believed the prayer meetings should be called only during certain phases of the moon. That seemed like superstition to us.

It was particularly dry in 1934. At the children's Christmas program in the village of Orloff several men decided to call a prayer meeting for the following evening. Many people came.

"Dear God," they prayed, "we know You love us. You brought us out of Russia. You have helped us here when we thought we could not go on. And now we pray for rain that we might have bread for our children. Give us this day our daily bread."

Then they went home to bed. At midnight brother Frank Wiens, who reported later, was awakened by a wonderful sound: it was raining. It rained all night. Next evening the villagers met again to thank God for answering their prayers.

Mr. Wilhelm Klassen, a man in our midst, has measured and recorded the rainfall since we first came. He has also recorded the dates of our meetings when we prayed for rain. He reports, for example, that when the severe drouth of 1952 did not end, a prayer meeting was held for rain. Light showers followed during the next two days, but on the fifth and seventh day after the prayers, heavy rains came. In 1953 we had three successive evenings of prayer for rain. Light showers followed on the first, second, and fourth days, heavy rains on the seventh and eighth days. According to his report, we again experienced a severe drouth in 1954. In the fourth month without rain we again had a prayer meeting. A light shower followed that same evening, and two days later we had a heavy rain.

Some here insist that these rains would have come anyway. "Prayer," they say, "cannot change the weather." But if God is Creator of the universe, and if He loves us, why can He not make His creation do His will to meet our need? I suppose there will always be those who believe prayer can bring rain and those who do not believe it. We cannot prove that prayer works except by faith.

PIONEERING IS DANGEROUS

In my paper I printed some stories about tigers and other wild animals. Actually we do not have tigers here, but jaguars. They are dangerous, and our men hunt them. Sometimes they tell jaguar stories that are hard to believe.

The jaguars do not bother us very much. Would you believe that grasshoppers are much, much worse? I remember a man telling me of an experience in the village of Rosenfeld. The sun was setting. Tired farmers were returning from their fields. The crops were almost ready to be harvested and looked very promising, especially the cotton. Suddenly someone said, "Look, rain is coming."

"No," said the others, "it can't be rain. We haven't had a north wind. It must be smoke." With dismay they suddenly realized that it was a cloud of grasshoppers.

"As far as I could see," a man said, "there were grasshoppers. Millions and millions of them. The sky was black. All the farmers and their children immediately grabbed basins and tin cans and beat on them to scare them away. But there were too many. I could not keep them out of my face. My dog pinched his tail between his legs and ran for shelter. The cows panicked and bellowed with fright. Even the chickens, which usually like to eat grasshoppers, were terrified. It was too much for them. All the while I could hear the grasshoppers eating, especially the kafir corn. Cornstalks and even tree branches broke under their weight. Some came into the house under the door. It was a bad night. By next morning most of them were gone. So was the cotton, and with it the hopes of the farmers for another year."

I must tell you, too, about getting lost in the Chaco. Do you know what it is like to be lost? In Europe there are so many people it is almost impossible to find an empty spot, but here it is easy to get lost, and very dangerous. We cannot survive long without water because of the heat.

Soon after we came to Paraguay, a nine-year-old boy, Cornelius, wandered away from the other pupils on a school picnic and became lost. "I wanted to find more cactus berries," he said later, "because the other boys had more. All at once I was alone. I called, but no one answered, and so I kept on walking. The path became narrower and narrower, so I turned back. I ran and ran. Then I saw

that the sun was setting. I was tired, so I lay down to sleep. But soon I was up again and ran some more. I heard animal noises all around me, but it was dark and I could not see them. Then I saw some water. I pulled out my *bombilla* (metal drinking "straw") and drank and drank. Then I ran again. And suddenly I saw a light. I whistled. Some soldiers approached with their guns pointed at me. When they saw I was a boy they asked, 'Are you a Menonita?' and I said '*Si.*' They gave me food, pulled the thistles out of my feet, and put me to bed. Then they brought me back home."

Little Jacob was not so fortunate. He followed his father as he brought the cows to pasture and suddenly disappeared. The whole village immediately turned out to search for him, including many Indians who knew the area well. Next day three Indians found him lying on a large cactus, dead. He had run about eight miles.

Not long ago two young men hunting for their mules lost their way. They were found six days later. One had just died, but the other recovered, though he was near death when they found him. They had lived on cactus berries, but had had nothing to drink. It turned out they were very close to a pond, but did not know it.

LIGHT TO THE INDIANS

I also want to tell you about our work with the Chaco Indians. Two large tribes —the Lengua and the Chulupi—live in this area. Now the Ayoreos, whom we call Moros, are also here. Further south, across the Pilcomayo River in Argentina, is the large Toba tribe. Further north are the Chamococos, but we see little of them.

The Indians were here when we came. They have probably been here for centuries. They didn't bother us. We gave them some food and gifts, and soon they were friendly enough to come into our villages. Some began to work for us, and we paid them in money and food. We also tried to learn their language, but they learned our Low German faster. It sounds strange to hear an Indian speak Low German. We taught them Bible stories and built a school for their children. They learned very quickly. One of them wrote this letter to his teacher, who had left for a time:

"My name is Hakuk amay. I am always lonely. I am lonely for my friend, the teacher. I have been asking when my friend the teacher is coming back. A Mennonite said, 'I don't know if he is coming back.' Then I was sad in my innermost. But now I am happy because I have heard that he is coming back. I am also glad because I want to study God's Word. Show my letter to the other Argentinians. I am glad that God takes care of me, and I trust Him."

Soon so many Indians came that our streets were always full of beggars. They had no other way to find food, it seemed. Some of our women were afraid of them because they come and go very quietly. One never knew when an Indian was looking in the window, or even standing behind one, just watching. They also took our names, in Low German, for themselves. Soon we had an Indian named *Yaash* (Jacob), *Yeeat* (George), *Tjnals* (Cornelius), *Peyta* (Peter), and many more. They particularly enjoyed watermelons, which grow very well in the Chaco. Often they would eat them till their stomachs bulged, and then they could not work. We Mennonites did not always treat them fairly.

After discussing with their chiefs and with the Indians who were already Christians how we could best help them, we decided together to settle them on land in villages much like our own. This is difficult and requires much patience on our part, too, because they have never lived in one place for any length of time. But the plan is working out well. They have schools and churches and good farms. Over fifteen hundred of them are now baptized Christians. They have taught us much about humility and simple faith in God. One of their chiefs gave the following speech not long ago:

"Brothers, I was a pagan and grew old among pagans. I know what that kind of life is like. Once a preacher came to us to show us that there is a God. And we said, 'Why, do you think we do not know that there is a God? Go back to where you came from.'

"Later another preacher came. He wanted to teach us that it is wrong to steal and to lie and to get drunk. And we said, 'You are a fool. Do you think we do not know that? But do you know it? Go home and teach it to your own people, who steal and lie and drink much more than we do.'

"After a time another Christian came to my hut. His name was Henry Pauch. He said, 'I have come to you in the name of Jesus to let you know that He loves you and died for you. He wants you to know that He became a man like you so He could help you find the way to God.' Then he lay down in my hut and fell asleep.

"I marveled at this man. He spoke so simply about love and peace. He said Jesus forgives me. And then he lay down and slept unafraid. I could have killed him, but he trusted me. And I said in my innermost, 'This is something else.' And when he awoke, I interpreted what he had said to my tribe and asked him to say more. That is how the grace of God came to the Lengua tribe."

The Indians have become our brothers

in Christ. A few years ago we began making contact with the Moros. They are wild and dangerous. One of our young men, Cornelius Isaac, made them his responsibility. He had been given a large scholarship to study at Canadian Mennonite Bible College in Winnipeg, but he finally turned it down. "I do not need more education to tell these poor Indians about Jesus," he said. But one day in 1958, while he was trying to be friendly to them, they drove a spear through him and killed him. Some of his last words in the hospital were a prayer that the Moros too might get to know Jesus. At his funeral three young men stood up and offered to continue the work, and today many Moros know Jesus as their friend and Savior. Perhaps that is why God brought the Mennonites into the Chaco—to be a light to the Indians, showing them the way to God.

*   *   *

That is the story of Nicolai Siemens, and through him, part of the story of the Mennonite pioneers in the Chaco of Paraguay. If you want to read more, you will need to learn German. That will open the door to a rich treasure house, the pages of the *Menno Blatt* where for twenty-five years Siemens told the story of faith and hope in his own beautiful way.

In 1950 Nicolai Siemens had a serious accident when the propeller of a plane in Filadelfia hit his arm. He had just handed the pilot a package of goodies for his grandchildren in Asuncion when he stepped back into the path of the propeller. But he recovered. He was the most cheerful man in the hospital.

A few years later he retired. He did not tell the new editor of the *Menno Blatt* how to do the work. He simply said, "Now it's your turn. May God bless you. Let me know if I can help."

Mr. Siemens died in 1958. At his funeral one speaker said, "It was clear to Nicolai Siemens that he had not come to the Chaco just by chance. He knew that God's almighty hand had brought him here. That is why he was always so cheerful and full of hope."

7

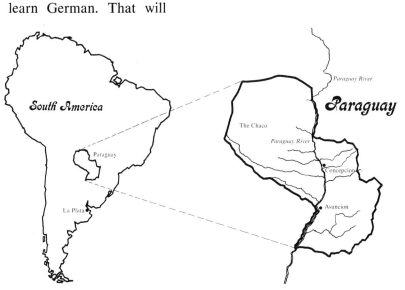

Harold S. Bender
1897-1962

"I am H. S. Bender, Dean of the Goshen College Biblical Seminary of Goshen, Indiana, and Chairman of the Peace Section of the Mennonite Central Committee, representing the Mennonite and affiliated churches of the United States numbering over one hundred forty thousand baptized members, who live in over half the states of the Union, from New York to California and Texas to Montana. It is on behalf of these churches, whose history goes back 425 years to Switzerland and Holland in Reformation times, and who began to come to this land in 1683, that I submit this statement to our elected representatives in the hope that it may contribute to a decision not to adopt the present bill or any other act providing for compulsory universal military training in any form."

The scene was a large and beautiful room in the Capitol Building in Washington, D.C., where members of Congress were meeting to plan military service for every young man in America. The date was March 1, 1955. The man who was speaking looked impressive indeed. He was of medium height, stocky, and well built. He wore a black suit and a plain coat without a tie. His hair was thin and grey. His face looked calm, intelligent, and determined; it was creased here and there by the hard work of many years and the burden of heavy responsibilities. He was clearly a man to be reckoned with.

"While I have come here to speak on behalf of all Americans and the welfare of the entire nation which we love and cherish," he continued, "I am not their spokesman. I speak rather for my own people whose memories include the bitter recollection of the experiences of their forefathers in those lands of Europe (Germany and Russia) where militarism won the day in the early 19th century, with its universal compulsory military training;—lands from which they fled to the freedom and liberty of a non-militarized America. My own experience is typical of many. My own grandfather just one hundred years ago fled from military service demands in Germany, and my wife's father did the same just short of seventy years ago. . . ."

Who was this man who stood before the leaders of the land like a prophet from the Old Testament? What made him do it, and why was he so convinced that war was wrong?

ELKHART, INDIANA

Harold S. Bender was born in Elkhart, Indiana, on July 19, 1897. His father, George, was a schoolteacher. He was also treasurer of the mission board and received thousands of dollars from the churches every year to send missionaries to foreign lands. Because of this interest

in telling others about Jesus Christ, his son Harold often talked of becoming a missionary to another land. He was indeed to become a missionary, even though he always lived in Indiana.

As Harold grew up he became an enthusiastic Hoosier. He loved northern Indiana with its beautiful lakes and its two rivers, the Elkhart and St. Joseph. He became very fond of the waving fields of wheat and the tall, long rows of corn. The orchards were a particular treat with cherries ripening first, then peaches, and finally apples. Apple cider was one of his favorite drinks. He particularly enjoyed spending time on the Miller farm helping with chores and other work. One day as he was driving a team of horses and a wagon with a large five-gallon can filled with cream on it, the horses became frightened and began to run. They ran through a ditch and almost upset the wagon. Harold just barely stayed on the seat. Finally he got them stopped, but the cream can had upset and the cream flooded the wagon, oozing to the ground from every crack and corner.

But Harold was not only interested in farm work. He wrote the following letter to his church story paper:

This is my first letter to the *Words of Cheer*. I like to read this nice little paper. I am eleven years old. I go to Sunday school every Sunday I can. I will answer some of the questions sent by the boys and girls. Jesus spoke the Beautitudes. They are found in Matt. 5. Noah was 120 years building the ark. The waters prevailed 150 days on the face of the earth. The shortest chapter in the Bible is Psalm 117. The first man to get intoxicated was Noah. Abel was the first man to ascend into heaven. The longest

chapter in the Bible is Psalm 119. The word 'seventeen' is found in Genesis 32:2. I will close with a few questions. Who built Nineveh? How many sons did Samuel have? What were their names? How did Cain know his offering was not accepted by the Lord? How many stalls did Solomon have for his horses? How many wives did Solomon have?

Yours truly,
Harold S. Bender

One day in the same year in which Harold wrote this letter, he faced a big decision in his fifth grade at the Fifth Ward School. Some of his classmates decided to play a practical joke on their music teacher, who was meek and timid. "Listen," they said before she came in. "When she comes we all behave as usual. When she strikes pitch on the piano, hum it. Okay?"

"Okay," the others said.

"And when she brings down her baton to start the singing," they continued, "we all keep quiet. Understand? Man, will she be embarrassed!"

They all agreed except Harold, who said, "No, fellows, that's no way to treat a teacher. . . ."

Before he could say any more, however, the teacher came into the room. Everything went as the class had planned until she brought down her baton. All were quiet except Harold, whose voice burst out loud and clear through all four lines of the verse until his classmates half-heartedly joined in, one by one.

Years later his regular fifth grade teacher recalled that "Harold was the most brilliant pupil I ever had."

He was also good at finding ways to earn money. Like many of his friends, he delivered magazines and newspapers:

The Elkhart Truth, The Country Gentleman, The Ladies Home Journal, and *The Saturday Evening Post.* He cut lawns and cleaned windows. He helped his father sell maple syrup which they shipped in from Pennsylvania. He also raised pigeons—too many pigeons, his mother thought.

One day she said, "Harold, look at all the pigeon dirt and feathers on our yard. It's blowing over to the neighbors, too. You're going to have to do something about it."

He did. Soon after, when Thanksgiving Day came, he supplied seventeen pigeons for the family dinner with friends.

It was at this time that Harold decided to tell the church openly about his faith in Jesus. He was baptized and became a member of the Prairie Street Mennonite Church in Elkhart.

A few years later, in 1914, he graduated from the Elkhart High School and entered Goshen College. There he was soon called "a herald of truth, a great defender." He enjoyed debating and singing. He also became a champion chess player. Because he needed money, he took one year out from college to teach school at Thornton, Indiana. He graduated from Goshen College in 1918, with a strong interest in history. Then he went to teach at Hesston College in Kansas.

ELIZABETH

Soon after his arrival at Hesston, Harold ran into trouble. It was the day for the annual freshman class outing to nearby Halstead, and he was class sponsor. But he had forgotten to buy a treat for the class, as was the custom.

"Andy," he said to his friend, "do you have a car?"

"Yes, I do," Andy replied. "I'm one of the drivers for the outing."

"Well, then," Harold responded, "take me to Newton while the others eat breakfast. Perhaps we can find a treat for the class in a store there."

So they drove to Newton. The town was quiet and most of the stores were still closed. As they walked up and down Main Street looking for a candy store or some place of business that was open, a big team of mules pulling an ice wagon came trudging leisurely up the middle of the street. There was no driver, and the reins were tied to the seat. Harold had never had anything to do with mules, and he thought they were running away.

"Andy," he said, "we've got to stop those mules. They're running away. The driver may be hurt."

"No, I don't think so," his friend answered. "I think they know where they are going and will probably stop at the next delivery point. Just leave them alone."

But Harold thought a team of mules should not be wandering around on Main Street without a driver, and decided to stop them.

"Whoa," he shouted, "whoa, whoa," but the mules paid no attention. Walking close behind them he grabbed for the reins, but got only one. Clutching the morning paper, which he had just bought, with one hand and jerking and pulling the rein with the other, he shouted again, "Whoa, whoa." When the old mule turned his head and saw the stranger with the paper in one hand, he became frightened and began to run. Now there was indeed a runaway team of mules on Main Street!

Harold was not about to give up something he set out to do. Holding the paper and the rein, he slid on his shoes for several blocks. In the meantime the driver made his appearance, his ice tongs hanging over his shoulder. Piercing the still morning air with his curses, he called to Harold, "Let them go! Let them go! For goodness sake, let them go!"

Harold could not hear him, however, because the wagon made so much noise. At the second street crossing the team turned right, all the time clattering down the middle of the street, with Harold still holding on.

Fortunately, a freight train standing across the street blocked the way, and the mules stopped of their own accord. Harold was glad to let them stand there for he was quite exhausted and his shoe soles were worn out.

Harold taught at Hesston College for two years and then went back to Goshen College to teach. There he became reacquainted with blonde, blue-eyed Elizabeth, whose father, John Horsch, was a well-known writer and historian in Pennsylvania. They had known each other casually as seniors, but things were different now.

Though they were both very busy teaching at the college, they still found time for each other. On a spring morning the college Glee Club, of which Harold was a member, left for Lima, Ohio, where they were to sing that evening. They took the train to Kendallville, Indiana, there to catch the electric train to Fort Wayne and Lima. But when they came to Kendallville, Harold, who was riding with Elizabeth, did not hear the conductor call out "Kendallville," and missed the stop. He got off at the next stop, Waterloo, and managed to catch another train to Lima, where he arrived just in time for the concert.

Harold and Elizabeth were married in a simple service on May 9, 1923, and left soon after for Germany, where Harold wanted to study for a year. Because Elizabeth was also interested in Menno-

nite history, they became a team of scholars. She worked with him for nearly forty years in this way, but also continued her teaching at the college. No one had ever seen a better team. They did everything together.

After they had returned to Goshen from Germany they often had students and friends over for dinner. They planned the menu together. Harold loved to go grocery shopping with Elizabeth, especially if they were expecting company. Sometimes they served oysters, sometimes chicken, sometimes chili. And ice cream. His friends often marveled at how much home-made ice cream Harold could eat. He was also fond of ketchup. Once Elizabeth said, "He eats ketchup on everything except his ice cream."

When their daughters, Mary and Nancy, were born to them, their joy was complete.

PEOPLE ARE IMPORTANT

Harold was asked to be dean of Goshen College, which meant planning the courses to be taught, as well as counseling students and professors. Students respected him and some were afraid of him. One day a student saw another student walk nervously back and forth in the hall.

"What's wrong?" he asked.

"I have to go in to see Dean Bender, and I'm afraid," the student replied. "I've walked up and down this hall for fifteen minutes trying to work up enough courage."

"Aw, just go on in," his friend answered. "You'll like him."

He did. "You know," he said later, "Dean Bender made me feel that he thought knowing me was a privilege and a blessing."

One of Harold's secretaries wrote: "His life said to me, 'People are important. They are more important than anything else, except God.' "

Students liked him most of all as a teacher, especially of church history. They could tell he loved the church. One day he told his students: "I hope this course will help you to love the church. But whether you do or not, I do. The church is the people of God."

To his students, the people they knew as members of the church often seemed no better than any other people. They knew, however, that Dean Bender was talking about what the church could be with the help of God's Spirit.

Harold knew what his students thought. He also believed that some of the churches were not what they should be. That is why he taught his students to love the church and to work with it. One Sunday morning, when he saw two students walk away from the college to attend another church, he drove after them and brought them back for the college church service.

Sometimes when he talked about the Mennonite Church he seemed to forget where he was. He would stand with his elbows on the lectern, his head in his hands and his eyes closed. Or he would walk back and forth in the classroom as though in another world. Once when he was talking about Felix Manz, one of the first Mennonites to die for his faith, he said, "I remember when on January 5, 1525, they took him down to the River Limmat in Zuerich, tied his hands behind his back, and threw him into the river."

These were the signs of a good teacher. He seemed to live the history of the church over and over in his own life.

"I took five courses under him one winter," a student said. "He was the greatest teacher I ever had."

Another confessed, "It was hard to take notes in his classes . . . because ev-

erything he said was important and meaningful. I just simply wrote as fast as I could."

Still another said of Harold, "It takes a great heart to take pity on those who are not as intelligent as you are. He took pity on me."

Because he had so much work to think about, Harold usually walked the campus sidewalks with his head down. He often picked up litter, but he did not seem to notice people when they passed by. Because of this, students called him the "absent-minded professor." But when they needed him he had time. After a visit in Dean Bender's office a student once said, "During those minutes I was the only person in the world who mattered to him." When students needed money Harold always found a way to help them. Often he gave them odd jobs around his house like mending the porch steps, sealing up the bathroom leaks, or changing the storm windows; and then he paid them for the work. Sometimes he advanced or gave them money out of his own pocket. On special occasions classes would meet at his home in the evening and then Elizabeth would serve pretzels and apple cider while they talked.

Other people traded cars, but the Benders kept on driving an old Dodge. "It still runs fine," Harold would say, or, "I need my money for other things." Those "other things" often turned out to be people in need. When he drove, he was so busy thinking or talking with his passengers that he didn't seem to notice he was driving an old car. Once a soft-drink truck nearly ran into him because his mind was somewhere else.

On another occasion, while driving from Goshen to Elkhart, he ran through several lights just after they had turned red. A friend who was with him was getting nervous and finally said, "Harold, did you notice that the last light was red?"

Harold replied, "Was it? I'm sorry. I guess the Lord is seeing us through."

The fuel gauge on his car always seemed to show "empty." "I'm an optimist," he would say. "I think we'll get there." He usually did.

WAR IS SIN

In the midst of all his activities a deep conviction had been growing in Harold's mind that war is sin. While still a student in Germany he had come to believe that to follow Jesus meant to love everybody, even your enemies. Soon after coming to Goshen College to teach, he had written to Elizabeth's father, "Several of us attended the pacifist (peace) conference at Manchester. It was the first time for me and very enlightening."

As Harold studied the life of his Mennonite forefathers he saw that they were men of peace. Jesus himself had said, "Blessed are the peacemakers, for they shall be called sons of God" (Mt. 5:9). To follow Jesus meant to be a peacemaker. To hurt and kill others was sin. War was sin because it destroyed people whom Jesus loved.

With this concern came a fear that war might soon break out with Germany. Would the Mennonite churches be ready to follow Christ then? And so he wrote an article for all to read, which he entitled, "In Time of Peace Prepare for War." "In Russia," he wrote, "the Mennonites were given exemption from military training on the basis of service rendered in forestry work. . . . This service was financed by the Mennonite Church. Must not some such plan be worked out and held in readiness to be proposed in time of war. . . ? Are we prepared for such an alternate service?"

A few years later, when the war seemed to come even closer, he wrote: "We believe that war is altogether contrary to the teaching and spirit of Christ and the gospel, that therefore war is sin . . . that it is wrong in spirit and method as well as in purpose, and destructive in its results."

He also wanted to prevent Christians from growing rich in times of war, and so he wrote, "We ought not to seek to make a profit out of war . . . which would mean profiting from the shedding of the blood of our fellow men." Christians, he believed, should use their money to bring "relief to the needy, or the spreading of the gospel of peace and love."

War did come. Thousands and thousands of people were killed by bombs and guns and fire. Harold was sad that some Mennonites took part in this, too, but he had indeed helped many more to see that Christ wanted His disciples to love and help others, not to destroy them. Christians must be willing to suffer, if necessary, rather than make others suffer. And so Mennonites worked in forests, in mental hospitals, on farms, and all over the world wherever needy people were found. The churches sent and supported these workers through the Mennonite Central Committee (MCC), an organization for helping others.

Harold traveled many miles, encouraging and helping MCC personnel. Once when he was far from home, he stayed with a family who had a three-year-old girl called Karen. At supper time, when the main dishes had been removed, Harold was the first to receive his dessert. He immediately began eating it. But Karen said, "Brother Bender, we wait until everyone is served before eating our dessert." Her parents were quite embarrassed, but he replied, "You are so right, Karen. I'm sorry, and thank you for reminding me."

BIENENBERG

One day when Harold was in Basel, Switzerland, he saw a beautiful Bible school. He turned to his friend, Hans, who was walking with him, and said, "Hans, this is the kind of school we need for Mennonites in Europe."

Hans replied, "That would be like reaching for the moon. Anyway, this school is not for sale."

"Then we must build one," said Harold.

Hans thought to himself: "Where does he think the money will come from, and the teachers, and the students?"

Today Hans is president of the board of trustees of a beautiful Bible school at Liestal, near Basel, called the "Bienenberg." There are fine buildings and teachers and students. Harold worked hard to build the school, but most of all it was his faith in God that made the dream come true. People trusted him. He made them want to do their best.

BIRD SKINS

When people needed help they often came to Harold. "He was a friend when I needed friends," one man said.

The Mennonites in Paraguay soon knew this, too. As secretary of MCC he had written letters to them and sent them money. They had been refugees and were therefore very poor. They needed to earn money. Noticing all the strange and lovely birds around them, birds they had never seen in Russia, they thought, "Perhaps we can send bird skins and feathers to Harold S. Bender to sell for us in the United States."

Soon Harold received a notice from the Treasury Department of the United States informing him that they were holding a package of bird feathers in customs for him. "My," thought Harold, "bird feathers! What shall I do with bird feathers? Who will buy them?" But he sent money to Paraguay for them out of his own pocket. That encouraged the Mennonites in Paraguay to send more. And more. Soon skins and feathers piled up in his office together with all his books about theology and history. Finally he wrote a letter to the national museum:

Goshen, Indiana
June 14, 1947

The Smithsonian Institute
Washington, D.C.

Dear Sirs:

. . . meanwhile, some shipments of bird skins from Paraguay have accumulated, and I am taking the liberty to ship them all to the Smithsonian Institute. . . . If you wish to pay me for any of these skins . . . I shall be very glad to receive it. I have already paid the collector for them. . . .

Sincerely yours,
Harold S. Bender

The museum took the skins and feathers, mounted them, and has them on display today.

LET US GO ON

Though all of these things kept Harold very busy, he always took time to work for peace. To do this he arranged many peace conferences in North America and Europe and participated in them. Once when he discovered Joseph Hromadka from a communist nation to be a sincere Christian for peace, he threw his arms around him and hugged him as a brother in Christ. In a speech at one of the peace conferences Harold, paraphrasing Hebrews 6:1, said, "Let us go on in a clearer vision of what we believe, in our understanding of the meaning of love, in our service and witness to all men, and in our working together for the Kingdom of God."

Harold knew that there would always be wars in the world because many men do not follow Christ. But he also knew that those who love Jesus have another way. "The teachings of Jesus and the power of the gospel," he wrote, "are the solution to the problems of sin in man and society. . . . The very cross of Christ itself, the heart of our faith . . . speaks against war. This is the cross which Christ has made our cross, the symbol and method of the Christian way of discipleship, of self-denial, and of suffering love."

When the atomic bomb, which could destroy the whole world, was developed, he wrote an article entitled, "A Serious Hour in World Affairs." "Are we ready," he asked, "to make clear [to the government] that we want no such protection . . . ? Can we escape a share of the guilt if we remain silent . . . ?" As a Christian he did not want others to be destroyed to keep him safe; he wanted life and faith and peace for all men.

This work for peace took him away from his home and family a great deal. But when he was home he was really at home, playing games with Mary Eleanor and Nancy, or taking Elizabeth shopping, since she did not drive the car. One evening, while he was waiting in front of a store for her, a policeman became suspicious. He walked up to Harold and said, "Who are you, Mister?"

Harold replied, "I am Harold Bender of Goshen College. Who are you?"

He particularly enjoyed baking a cake on Sunday afternoons. The richer the cake, the better he thought it was. And then he would be off again to catch a train or plane.

Once, after he had almost missed a train because he needed more files and letters from his office, his secretary said with a sigh, "I feel like a mother who has just gotten ten children off to school in the nick of time."

His last great conference was in Kitchener, Ontario. Nearly twenty-five thousand Mennonites had gathered there for the Seventh Mennonite World Conference. Harold was president of the conference. He had given much time to its work, and he loved it. As he closed the conference with prayer he knew it would be the last time, for he was very ill. "Almighty, eternal, and everlasting God," he prayed, ". . . our hearts are full of desire to praise Thee and to adore Thee, and to say: Thou art our God, Thou art our Father. Thou hast been with us. We thank Thee for the brethren. Increase our love for the brethren and for the brotherhood . . . help us to help one an-other . . . and grant that we shall so live that men may see it is the Lord whom we love and whom we serve." Those who were there will never forget that prayer.

He died soon after, leaving Elizabeth to continue some of the work which they had done together for so many years. Over a thousand people attended the funeral service in the Goshen College Church. They sang one of the hymns Harold had loved very much: "Lift Your Glad Voices." It told of those who die in faith as being alive with Jesus forever, because Jesus himself is alive:

> *Lift your glad voices in triumph on high,*
> *For Jesus hath risen, and man shall not die;*
> *Vain were the terrors that gathered around Him,*
> *And short the dominion of death and the grave.*
> *He burst from the fetters of darkness that bound Him,*
> *Resplendent in glory, to live and to save:*
> *Loud was the chorus of angels on high,*
> *The Savior hath risen, and man shall not die.*
> *The Mennonite Hymnal, No. 175*

8

Ngongo David

I was born into the Bapende tribe near Nyanga, Zaire, in the heart of Africa. My father was an important man in the tribe, a *pungu* (assistant) of the village chief. There were no Christians in our village. My father had many idols, but he was very much afraid of spirits. He said spirits were all around us, waiting to hurt us. At night, when the fire burnt low, our family would sit close together because we were afraid. Often my father put flour on the ground for the spirits. He whitewashed my hands to keep spirits from harming me. Sometimes he killed a chicken, took the insides out, and spread them on the ground as a sacrifice to the spirits. He believed that then the spirits would leave little children alone.

One day, when I was still a little boy, my father heard that my uncle was coming to get me. My uncle was in deep trouble in his own village, and the elders said he would need to give a *muthu* (person) to settle the matter. In my country children do not belong to their father, but to their mother and her family. Since my mother had died, her brother, my uncle, could claim me. When he was told by the elders that he must give a person to the man he had wronged, he decided to give me.

When my father heard of it he was very angry. According to our customs there was nothing wrong with what my uncle wanted to do, but I was the only

son of my father's favorite wife, and he loved me very much. He cut a big gash into his arm. With the blood he painted red lines of war on his temples and forehead. He found a long bird's feather and stuck it in his hair over his right ear. He told me to stay close to the house. Then he sat down before the door on our little bamboo stool with his loaded gun across his knees and waited for my uncle to come.

He sat there many days. He ate and slept very little. Then word came that my uncle had heard about my father's anger and had changed his mind. He would not come to get me. We were happy. My father was a powerful man.

After a time we heard that a man from the Muluba tribe was telling stories to children under a huge tree in the clearing across the stream. My father said I could go to hear him, too. The stories were about a man named Jesus and a man named Paul. The storyteller said his own name was Makusudi Paul. He taught us strange new songs and made funny little marks on a piece of board. He called it writing. I had never seen such things before.

One day Makusudi said, "Today we are going to do something new. We are going to talk to Nzambi (God). Everyone must bow their heads, close their eyes, and be very quiet while I speak to Him." But when he began speaking to the spirits we all became very afraid.

I peeked through my fingers and saw his eyes were closed. Quickly I turned around and tiptoed out of the clearing. The others followed. When we were in the forest we ran as fast as we could. We did not want the spirit to whom he was talking to get us. Makusudi must have been surprised when he opened his eyes and found himself all alone under the big tree.

But next day we came back again. It was good to learn about Jesus from the Big Book. Soon I could write my name —Ngongo.

A white man and his wife came to help Makusudi. I had not seen many white men before. They built a school, and I helped as much as I could. Then my father died, and I stayed with "the mission," as we called it, to help there all the time.

WHEN DID I BECOME A CHRISTIAN?

After many months Mr. Valentine, the white man, asked me to go along with him on a tour of the villages far away. We met many people. I had never been so far away from home. Day after day Mr. Valentine preached to the people about Jesus and His love, and some believed what he said. One day, while he was preaching about how God's Spirit had spoken to Saul on the Damascus road, I felt the Spirit speaking to me, too, and I said "yes" to God. I became very happy. I told God I now belonged to Him. I prayed and knew God was hearing me, too.

When we returned from our long journey I received further instruction in the Christian faith and then I was baptized and joined the church. I took David as my new name, just as Saul took Paul as his name when he became a Christian. God called David to be king when he was young and used him in a great way.

I was young, too, and God wanted to use me. So my name is now Ngongo David.

Then another great thing happened to me—I got married. As a Christian I knew I wanted only one wife, and I wanted to love her like Christ loves the church. God sent me Mitoro, who had taken the name Ruth when she became a Christian. She is now called Mitoro Ruth. Ours was the first Christian wedding in Nyanga. Our marriage certificate says that I would not beat Mitoro as a non-Christian husband does. I would eat with her, when at home, which he does not. A non-Christian man is the master in his house and eats by himself. His wife eats with the children in the kitchen. He treats his wife like a servant-slave, but Mitoro and I were partners together for God.

God kept working in my life. He made it possible for me to attend Bible school for three years. Our class met early in the morning. Every afternoon we went into the villages to tell people about Jesus Christ and to teach songs and Bible stories to the little children. When the three years were over, I was put in charge of a school of my own and was also responsible for preaching the gospel in eleven other villages. I was very busy, and God blessed my work. Soon my students became my helpers. Mayele Isaac and Musoko Philip were especially helpful.

I KNOW GOD LOVES ALL TRIBES

When things were going very well here, the church said they needed me to start a new work along the Loange River among the Bachoke people. I took it as a call from God, and went. I had a great longing to tell other tribes the good news of Jesus, too. It was hard work. To visit all the places where I had workers meant two hundred miles of bicycle travel over dangerous forest roads. I traveled those two hundred miles many, many times. God kept me safe from robbers and wild animals. Later the mission provided me with a car, but it gave out, and I bicycled again. I did this for eleven years.

One day Mitoro Ruth died and went to be with Jesus. I did not shout and moan like the non-Christians do when someone dies. I thanked God that she was now with Jesus, where I would be too one day. She left me with eleven children. I could not do my work and take care of them, but friends from the church helped. They said I should marry again because of my children. I said I would leave it in the hands of God.

After some years Frank Enns, my missionary friend, said he had heard of a fine Christian widow who was living in Tshingila village in the Bapende region. On our next gospel tour we came to this region and asked about her faith and life. I asked how she had acted when her husband died—like a Christian, or like a heathen? Everyone said, "She is a fine Christian woman. She has a loving heart for children, but has none of her own." So the evangelist and I went to visit her together. Her name is Lufeto Marianne. I told her all about myself and my family, and asked whether she would marry me. Her relatives discouraged her. I gave her five hundred francs and some salt, and promised to come back on our return journey. When I came back she said, "Yes," and followed me. She is a wonderful wife and a loving mother to my children.

When my oldest son died, his wife moved into our home, too. She has seven children, so we are a big family. But the children are growing up and leaving home. We live in a mud brick house with five rooms. It has a cement floor in it. Most of our windows have shutters instead of glass. We have ten pigs, three goats, and many chickens. We also have a big garden. We sell vegetables to the stores in Tshikapa and to men working in the diamond mines.

YOU ASK ABOUT PRAYER

We learned to pray more than ever before when independence came to the Congo in 1960. Suddenly the Belgian government was gone and there was much confusion. There were many leaders and no unity. Then the revolution came. All the white men were in danger of being killed, as well as many of us. We told the missionaries to leave. One morning they gave me the keys to all the buildings at Nyanga station, including their own houses, and fled across the border into Angola. We were thankful they were not killed as many others were. We prayed much for them.

When the missionaries went, they left their hunting guns here. I took them to the attic of the big house, together with all the ammunition, and hid them. When fighting started, the village people came and asked for the guns of the missionaries. I said, "No, they are not yours. Besides, you want to use them to kill people, but the Bible says that is a great sin."

Then they brought a man to me who was dying because his arm had been cut off by the enemy. They said, "Give us the guns or we will chop your arm off, too."

I said, "No. You can kill me if you wish, but I will not give you the guns to kill other people."

They left and said they would come back in the morning to kill me.

My friends told me to give the guns to the people. When night came I hid. I prayed all night. I sang my favorite song softly to myself over and over as part of my prayer for help:

What a friend we have in Jesus,
All our sins and griefs to bear;
What a privilege to carry
Everything to God in prayer!
O what peace we often forfeit,
O what needless pain we bear,
All because we do not carry
Everything to God in prayer.

Have we trials and temptations?
Is there trouble anywhere?
We should never be discouraged:
Take it to the Lord in prayer!
Can we find a friend so faithful,
Who will all our sorrows share?
Jesus knows our every weakness;
Take it to the Lord in prayer!

Are we weak and heavy laden,
Cumbered with a load of care?
Precious Savior, still our refuge,
Take it to the Lord in prayer!
Do thy friends despise, forsake thee?
Take it to the Lord in prayer!
In His arms He'll take and shield
*   thee,*
Thou wilt find a solace there.

Joseph Medicott Scrivent, 1885

93

I knew I was doing the will of God. He gave me peace and courage. He helped me. The men did not return in the morning. My friends said, "Ngongo David has a strong heart." It was an answer to prayer.

Those were hard days. The missionaries were gone and I was responsible for everything—the school, the church services, visiting the sick, and also caring for the mission property. The rebels came to steal and to kill. We never knew when they might kill us, too. Refugees came asking for help. Many people said we were spies and traitors because we were Christians. The members of our churches were scattered all over what was then called the Congo. Those were hard times.

Because I am honest I will tell you the hardest experience of all. It hurts my heart, but I will tell it. Was the hardest experience meeting the rebels who threatened to kill me? No. Was it all the work and responsibility? No. It was discovering that my own son had been stealing mission property and leading a bad life. I cried many bitter tears of shame and sorrow. I confessed it all to the church and asked forgiveness for my failure. He was my son. Then we voted to remove him from church fellowship and place him under church discipline so that he might repent and be restored to faith.

A Kipende proverb tells about a hunter who went out to hunt game. Soon he found a herd of antelope. He crawled closer and closer. Suddenly he stepped on a stick. It broke, and the noise it made scared the antelope away. He caught nothing. Sin in our lives is like a stick. It scares people away from faith in Jesus.

But in all this God heard my prayers. We learned to trust Him more. When the missionaries returned, they said we had grown strong and free in spirit. They said they would no longer be our leaders in the mission; we should lead and they would help us as we had earlier helped them. We agreed because we knew we needed each other and loved each other.

The new responsibility brings many burdens and trials. When fire catches my finger I put it in my mouth. The saliva kills the fire and relieves the pain. So when I get into a hot place I go to Jesus. He puts out the fire and relieves the pain in my heart. He hears and answers my prayers.

You Ask about My Work Now

I am an old man now, but I am still working in the church. It is getting harder for me to ride my bicycle for many miles. The Evangelical Mennonite Church of Zaire has asked me to be the president for some years now. Younger men do the traveling I used to do. But I am also still a pastor. A pastor must be a servant of the people. When they come to visit me I give them my chair to sit on.

We often say too many words of our own and do not use enough the Word of God. Another Kipende story tells about a bird that laid its eggs in a nest in a huge tree. People walked under the tree every day. The little bird sang, "People don't have eyes, people cannot see. They cannot even see my nest." But one day a man heard the song and saw the nest. He climbed the tree and killed the little birds in the nest. Then the mother bird sang, "My singing words have killed my little birds." So our own words often cause us trouble, but the good words of God give us life.

There are three Mennonite conferences in Zaire. Ours, the Evangelical Mennonite Church, has twenty-four thousand believers. The South Kasai conference has seven thousand, and the Mennonite Brethren conference has about ten thousand. So all together we are over forty thousand believers in the Mennonite churches of Zaire. We have many young people. Our biggest work is teaching over thirty-five thousand children in our schools every day. They are taught Bible together with all the other subjects. There are over a thousand students in secondary (high) schools. We have Bible schools and a new school of theology (seminary).

The churches of North America are helping us very much. We are brothers and sisters in Christ. They keep over seventy missionaries here to work with us in the schools, in evangelism, radio work, agriculture, and medical work. They send us young people to teach in our schools and to work with the poor. They send us money and supplies. Best of all they love us and pray for us.

Our churches consist of many strong Christians but also of some who are weak. When chickens are small they stay with the mother hen. But when they grow bigger they run away and do what they want to do. Then the hawk gets them. So Satan catches Christians who do not stay close to Jesus and the fellowship of His people. The missionaries brought a song which I love very much. Mrs. Frank Enns translated it for me.

It goes like this:

Anywhere with Jesus I can safely go;
Anywhere He leads me in this world
*   below;*
Anywhere without Him dearest joys
*   would fade;*
Anywhere with Jesus I am not
*   afraid.*

Anywhere! anywhere! Fear I cannot
*   know;*
Anywhere with Jesus I can safely go.

Anywhere with Jesus I am not
*   alone;*
Other friends may fail me, His is still
*   my own;*
Though His hand may lead me over
*   dreary ways,*
Anywhere with Jesus is a house of
*   praise.*

Jessie B. Pounds, 1861-1921

A Kipende proverb says, "A goat that follows two masters will get caught by the leopard." Christians have one Master, Jesus, and they follow only Him.

I have had many, many experiences. When I think of this I think of my favorite text: "All that happens to us is working for our good if we love God and are fitting into His plans" (Rom. 8:28). If I could talk to all the children who will read my story I would tell them about Samuel. He heard the call of God when he was young and said, "Here I am." He was not too young to serve the Lord. God uses children, too.

A few years ago the churches of North America invited Tshilembu Nicodeme and me to visit them. We flew very high and very fast. New York is a huge village. When I saw television for the first time in New York, I was frightened.

When I visited the churches in North America I told them: You are the fathers and mothers that have given birth to the Mennonite Church in Zaire. A father and mother that have given birth to a child have their eyes and ears directed toward it; they care for it, strive to rear it well, and hear its cries. You have brought us to our independence as a Church. But let us now draw together and help each other to carry forward the weight of the sacred work of Jesus. We are going ahead, but don't leave us to ourselves. I am thankful that God has given us so many brothers in other lands —in Africa and around the world in North America, in Europe, Asia, and South America.

There are many wild animals in Zaire —lions, wild boars, antelope, buffalo, hippos. If I wait too long to shoot when I go hunting, the animals run away or come to attack me. In either case I remain without food. I told the churches it is like that if we wait too long to go to Jesus when we are hurt deep inside. We will have more trouble and forget our love for Him.

When a woman has a gourd on her head we know that she is going to the river to get water. When people are Christians we know that they are followers of Jesus Christ.

9

Lena Graber

"Dear Home Folks,

"Today is a lovely cool day. I have not minded the weather yet at all. . . . But it is very dry and dusty, and such red dust! It reminds me of the dust of Utah. The gardens are still producing and many flowers are still blooming. The mango tree near the nurses' bungalow has new leaves and I guess will bloom soon. The oleander behind my bungalow is so beautiful now. The poinsettias are still blooming a little. I enjoy all the trees and plants. . . .

"I have been over at the hospital a few times already. On Monday afternoon I scrubbed with Dr. Yoder and Dr. Singh for a major abdominal operation. It was fun, but quite a bit different from what I have been used to. Ha! . . . Then yesterday I helped operate on a cancer of the heel, and put in a drain in a nasal sinus of a baby. This morning I went over right after breakfast to morning prayers and ward rounds. That was quite an experience to see the patients in the wards! I felt pretty low when I got back, but I must get over it. Perhaps when I can really start working I may be able to help certain things become better. . . . But I am so conscious of the need to know the language. I became aware of this as soon as I left the United States. . . . I am getting a Pundit [teacher], starting next week, for one hour a day to begin with. . . . I just must learn to talk.

"I have gotten quite a few insect bites since I am here. I don't think they are mosquitoes, but they may be fleas. They look like flea bites. I get them from the dogs around here, I think. . . .

"On Friday evening Dr. Yoders came by for me and we went to the Beares for dinner. And such a dinner! We ate in the back yard and it was so lovely. . . . They are interesting people to visit with. Mr. Beare was teasing Mrs. Beare with some snake eggs he had found. They are about the size of pigeon eggs. He has them in a fish bowl in her flower room. He is anxious to see what kind of snakes they will be.

"Yesterday morning I worked over at the hospital. . . . Before I had time to drink tea, two women came to the bungalow and asked me to come and help a woman who couldn't have her baby. My stomach turned one summersault and then I got ready and went over. . . . It took a long time. It was 9 o'clock when we sat down to supper. Well, it was all quite an experience for me. We had to work a while with the baby to make it breathe. Imagine how I felt when I helped to put the mother on a stretcher. I let the old aunt carry the baby while I carried the lantern out to the ward. There among a lot of all kinds of patients we put her on an old bed and laid the baby at her side. They all seemed happy, for the baby was a boy. After supper I took the lantern and went out again to see that she was alright. . . .

"I've just had a nice nap now. I really needed it because all the neighborhood dogs kept me awake last night. . . . I sleep on the veranda, and they raced back and forth under my bed. I tried to scare them but they wouldn't listen. . . . If I would have had a stick I would have reached out from under my [mosquito] net and hit them a good crack. I'm no friend to the dogs because their fleas are still biting me.

"I forgot to tell you about a woman who came in Saturday morning. She had her face all covered with her sari, and another woman was talking for her. She wanted and needed attention, but refused to let Dr. Yoder examine her [because he was a man]. So I took her in the treatment room and examined her. . . . Then I told Dr. Yoder, and he wrote the prescription. She really needed a minor operation but refused. So we gave her some more medicine. This all seems so queer. Then, too, the nurses won't wash out anything with blood or excreta on it. The dressings seem to have to be put on the floor in the wards until the sweeper picks them up. I must learn to understand them all and learn all the names of the compounders and nurses and just who is to do what. After that all I'll need to do is to see that it gets done. Ha! . . .

"Good night, and love to all."

Lena

By now you will have guessed that Lena is a nurse, but where was she and what was she doing when she wrote this letter?

A GIRL FROM IOWA

Lena Graber was born on April 28, 1910, on a farm in Wayland, Iowa. She enjoyed the farm, especially the chickens. She liked to feed and care for them and gather the eggs. But she was afraid of the big animals. Sometimes she had to milk the cows, but not if she could get out of it.

There were nine children in the Graber family, seven girls and two boys. Joe and Chris, the two boys, took great pains to stand by each other. After all, it was two boys against seven girls. So they invented a secret language which they called Grabish. No one else could talk or understand it. They began by spelling every word backwards. Then they learned to pronounce it that way. When one of their sisters began to understand a word, or even a sentence, they changed it. To tease the neighbors, they sometimes talked to each other in Grabish on the party-line telephone. Most people listened on the party line when the telephone rang. That was how they found out what was going on in the community. But when Joe and Chris talked, they couldn't understand a word. They didn't like it.

Lena enjoyed school. It was a small one-roomed country school with all eight grades taught by one teacher. They were like one big family. The older pupils were expected to help the younger ones with their lessons since the teacher could not possibly take care of all of them at one time. Lena liked to help others. By the time she was eleven she had finished grade eight, except for the final examinations.

"Lena," her father said, "I do not want you to graduate. You would have to leave home to go to high school, and you are too young for that."

"But, Daddy," she replied, "what shall I do then? You don't need me at home."

"Well," her father replied, "why don't you go back to school and help the teacher with the younger children? You could learn a lot that way. Besides, there are library books in school."

"Not very many," she answered, "and I've read most of them."

But she did go back—for two more years of grade eight. The teacher was very happy for her good help. Then she wrote the exams and went on to high school.

It was in high school that Lena began to think seriously about what she should do with her life. She had given her life to Jesus and wanted to follow Him, but what did that mean?

"My sister is a teacher," she thought to herself, "and father wants me to be a teacher, too. I wonder why?"

The more she thought about it, the less she liked the idea. One day her sister was ill and Lena took her place teaching all eight grades. That brought back memories of the three years she had spent in grade eight. In the evening her father came to get her with his horse and buggy.

"Well, Lena," he asked, "did you have a good day? Do you think you want to be a teacher now?"

"No, Father," she replied, "this settles it. I'm just not made to be a teacher. I think I will become a nurse. I like hospitals and helping people who are sick. But first I need to go to college."

Becoming a Nurse

The years at Goshen College in Indiana went by too quickly. Lena enjoyed all the fun and friends; she also enjoyed her studies, especially science and languages. After she had completed college, she attended the School of Nursing at the Mennonite Hospital in Bloomington, Illinois. Because she particularly liked to work with mothers and their babies, she specialized in obstetrics. She was a good nurse, and when the hospital asked her to stay on after graduation she con-

sented. She had reached her goal. Now she could settle down and enjoy her career.

But a very different life was waiting for her. In 1939, soon after she graduated, the second World War broke out. Armies marched and fought in Europe, Africa, and Asia. City after city was destroyed, and the people who survived became homeless refugees. It seemed as though men wanted to destroy the whole human race.

Far away from Europe, in Illinois, USA, Lena followed the activity of the war with an anxious heart.

"When people suffer," she said to herself, "they need nurses to help them, especially Christian nurses who can also help to heal their broken spirits. I wonder whether there is anything I could do to be of help?"

One day she read that the service agency of her church, the Mennonite Central Committee (MCC), was calling for volunteers, including nurses, to work with refugees in Egypt and Palestine.

"Lord, God," she prayed, "is this what you want me to do? I don't want to be here if you want me there."

The feeling that she should go became stronger. She sent in her name and waited for instructions.

Not long after making this decision she read an article by a missionary, Dr. Yoder, in which he described the great medical needs of the people in India and asked for nurses to come and help him.

"Because my father was a minister we entertained many missionaries in our home when I was a child, and so I had always been interested in missions," Lena confessed later. "I enjoyed the missionaries and their stories. In 1925 my brother Joe went to India and kept sending back interesting reports of his work. But I never thought I would be a missionary. I thought I just did not have what it took. Missionaries had to be very special people, I thought, and I was just an ordinary nurse. And then, quite unexpectedly, I received a letter asking whether I would go to India under the mission board instead of to Egypt under MCC, and I said yes. It seemed to be what God wanted me to do."

DHAMTARI CHRISTIAN HOSPITAL

Lena sailed on a small Portuguese ship to Lisbon and then to Bombay. On the ninth day out of New York she wrote, "Nine days out and six days seasick. . . . I was OK until Sunday 4 p.m. when we hit breakwater. From then on I couldn't keep a thing down until Wednesday. . . . Friday I tried to get up but couldn't. Sunday I tried to get up but couldn't. Today I got dressed lying down and so I got up on deck. I'm not going down to meals or I'll be in bed again. I am eating crackers and salted peanuts. . . ."

In Lisbon Lena waited many weeks for a ship to Bombay. The war made travel very difficult and dangerous. But finally she did sail, and on March 4, 1945, she wrote from India: "I had a nice trip. . . . From Bombay I went by train. I had gotten a bedding roll in Bombay, so I used it to sleep on. The train went about sixteen miles an hour. I enjoyed the scenery. . . . The most beautiful scene was a large woods with some kind of trees in full bloom in brilliant red. . . ."

It did not take Lena long to get to work at the hospital after she arrived in Dhamtari.

"Dear Es," she wrote to her sister Esther. "You ought to see the lame and the halt and blind come to the hospital each day. They seem so dried up that you wonder if they will be able to get up and walk home again. . . . They come with cancers, huge hernias, blindnesses of all kinds, scabies (itch), impetigo, tuberculosis, abscesses, etc. Some women won't let the doctor examine them, so I do it. And the babies! You are not surprised that they have a fifty percent infant mortality. There is simply nothing to feed the babies if there is no mother's milk. Some can afford a goat, but most cannot."

One week later she wrote again. "It seems I do not have time for letters except on Sunday. . . . We have done a lot of surgery since I am here. We have had twenty-one operated eyes and a lot of other big cases. We have had two cholera cases—both died. We cannot keep them here. We put them under the leper treatment roof. . . . They were pulseless when they came. We all took cholera shots again. . . ."

Lena wanted to learn the Hindi language as quickly as possible. "I am studying language each day. . . . I know most of the single letters. Over at the hospital I try the words I know, but then I get a whole bunch back [from the patients] that mean nothing to me. I'll demonstrate what I can write:

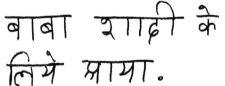

[The little boy came to the wedding.]

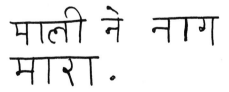

[The gardener killed a snake.] Several weeks later she wrote, "I sang Hindi words in church for the first time last Sunday."

WORMS, SPIDERS, AND SNAKES

The hospital was not Lena's only concern. She wrote: "One day this week a certain kind of worms hatched out. They came into the house, crawled all over the veranda. They only lasted three days, for which we were glad. Now I suspect some day soon we will have a crop of winged animals from them. . . ."

Lena was very brave when it came to insects, animals, and crawling things. Nurses do not let little things bother them, she believed. "You ought to see the huge spiders here," she wrote. "Last week I killed two in my room that were two inches wide (I mean from the end of the legs). You almost felt as if you were killing a little mouse. This morning as I pulled out a book to read, a big one crawled out. I'll draw a picture of how big they are. I can hear jackals every night."

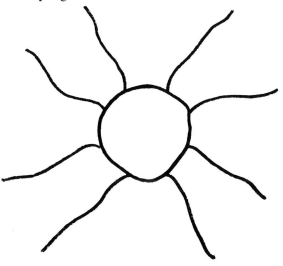

A little later she wrote: "Last week when I was out at Balodgahan I heard all kinds of snake stories. That night every time I woke up I thought I heard one crawling. One time I had to get up for the bathroom. I heard something up in the corner of the veranda so I decided to flash my flashlight up to see what it was. And just that quickly a bat flew at me. . . . Then last Monday evening they started on snake stories again. Mrs. Lapp told of how she put her shoes on one morning and her foot wouldn't go in, so she took it out again and the coils of a snake came back out of her shoe. I was glad I already had acquired the habit of shaking out my shoes before putting them on. I haven't seen any scorpions yet. . . ."

OF LOVE AND MERCY

But Lena was too busy to worry long about snakes and spiders. "Since I am business manager [of the hospital] and nursing superintendent," she wrote, "there are lots of things for me to do. We have three new compounders (male nurses) and I have to see that they know what to do. I spent a whole morning showing one how to take temperature and pulse. He does real well now. Then I help with supplies, handle the money, and keep the books. Then, too, I am teaching ethics and hygiene to the compounders. There is no textbook available, so I am writing my own lessons on the typewriter with carbons. Besides this there are 101 other things to do. Sometimes I wonder whether I am doing the work of a nurse. Anyway, we are very busy at the hospital. . . . I believe we had about 125 outpatients today."

The months passed by very quickly. Before she realized it another hot season had come, and with it the time for a vacation in the cool mountains. She wrote from Landour: "From here when you look northeast you see the whole Himalayan range covered with snow. Then when you look south you can see the plains. It is so nice and cool up here that I can hardly imagine really how hot Dhamtari is now. We came up the last week of April. Between Nagpur and Delhi it was terribly hot. The fever thermometer in my suitcase went up to 110 degrees. We are at 7500 feet elevation here. Right now the rhododendron trees are blooming. . . .

"The other day I saw some monkeys here. Five of them ran across my path and down the bank. Then they stopped to look at me and I looked at them. They chattered something to each other, and since I couldn't understand them I decided I'd better move along for fear they were plannning something to do to me. Ha!"

Back at the hospital after vacation, she wrote, "Just had a meal of dal-bhat and curry. I surely do enjoy Indian food . . . . You'd laugh if you would see how much rice I can eat now. You remember I didn't care much for it. . . ."

One of the things that troubled Lena most was the suffering that people experienced because they did not know some of the simple rules of hygiene. She remembered how she had learned as a child never to put anything except her elbow into her ear. "A case we had this morning almost turned my stomach," she wrote. "They brought in a baby of about eight months with an ear infection. The doctor ordered a basic ear wash, some ear drops, and some pills. I was busy with other work, so I sent Chamarin to wash it out. Pretty soon she came in all excited and told me there was something in the ear and she couldn't wash it out. So we brought the child into the operating room and the doctor began digging out what was in the ear. What do you think it was? Clam shells! They were ground up real fine and the ear was stuffed full of them. After the doctor had dug a hole through it, out rolled the pus . . . . I surely felt sorry for the baby who has to suffer all this because of the parents' ig-

norance. I told them never to put anything in the baby's ear unless the doctor tells them to. Then they answered *kya kare?* which means 'what to do?' "

Another case told the same story. "Yesterday evening we did a leg amputation. . . . It was on a young girl about sixteen years old. She was brought in a week ago with gas gangrene of the foot and leg . . . of course the leg was dead part of the way up already. . . . It seems she had a very difficult delivery and then a few days later the leg got terribly swollen. Someone burned it with a red hot sickle and then put on who knows what. I suppose the germs got in by that treatment. It seems terrible to think that now she will have to live with one leg just because of what was done through ignorance. She is such a pretty girl. . . ."

The hospital efforts to teach health did bring some results. It almost stopped the opium poisoning of children. "There were a lot of opium poisoned cases when I first came," Lena reported. "In the morning before they went into the fields, parents would give it to their children to keep them drowsy and quiet all day. Often when they brought them to the hospital later the children were nearly dead, just breathing about three times a minute. And their pupils would be pinpoint, their skin dry, their eyes sunken in. We would immediately begin treatment with fluids, drops, and particularly oil in their eyes because the cornea was sometimes so dry that it cracked. Some recovered, but some did not because their kidneys had been damaged by the dehydration. When we had done everything we could for the child we would turn to the people who were watching us (there are always many), and begin teaching them the simple rules of health. This has helped a great deal. By now we have very little opium poisoning."

The work of the hospital was made particularly difficult because many people were so poor. Babies were brought in barely alive because of malnutrition. If a mother did not have milk for her baby it often died. Once Lena wrote in desperation, "I am trying by hook or by crook to get more dried milk for the babies. . . . I wish the American army would give me a few fifty-pound barrels of the stuff."

Often the poor also suffered because they were outcasts from society through the caste system. "One woman is out under the tree," she wrote one day. "I put a round bamboo mat over her head . . . . She belongs to the caste that is outcaste and so cannot stay in the room of the hospital with the others. The others represent three castes, but all of equal status, so there is no trouble."

Often Lena and the hospital staff could not help because they were called too late. Once she wrote: "The day before yesterday they took the motor . . . to get a very sick patient at Mangal Terai . . . . Well, by the time they got there she just breathed her last. So they stayed and had the burial. . . . She had delivered twin boys. . . . So they wrapped up the babies and laid them on the back seat of the motor and brought them here. We kept them going until yesterday forenoon. One died at 9 A.M. and the other at 12 noon. . . . We laid them into a small packing box and buried them in the cemetery. The father had not come along because he had other children and his fields to look after. We felt bad that we could not save them, but I guess it is best this way without a mother."

Lena enjoyed the worship services in the church, even though in the beginning she could not understand anything. It did not take her long to understand, and then speak, Hindi. She used all of her vacation to study it. It was not long until she was asked to teach a Sunday school class. She described a special service in one of her letters: "We had comunion here last Sunday. I washed feet with one of the nurses. Here they not only wash your toes but the whole leg. And they get fresh water for each person. They have water in a big fifty-gallon tin and you just dip out of it."

The lepers, as they were called, who suffered from Hansen's disease, were a particular concern to the personnel of the hospital, and to Lena also. "The leper injections are quite hard to give," she once wrote. "I'm developing quite a muscle from giving them." Sports Day was a great occasion for the lepers, even though many had lost their fingers or hands and feet. Lena enjoyed every minute of it and told about it in another letter:

"On Friday afternoon we all went to Shantipur to the Sports Day put on by the lepers. . . . They had several races. One was a competition by four blind people to see who could walk up and hit a water pot. . . . Another was a stone gathering by fingerless patients. . . . Then they had six young leper women in a race. They carried full water pots on their heads and ran a certain distance. They had a guava-eating race by the boys. This caused a lot of laughter. The last was a tug-o-war between two sets of leper men. . . . Oh yes, I forgot, the leper men also did a stick dance. Joe can explain this to you, for he learned it when he was in Shantipur. They told me he is the only missionary who ever mastered it. It is complicated. . . ."

The years passed by. Lena came home once for a vacation and then returned again. The people learned to love Nurse Graber very much. She felt deeply with them in their pain and suffering. Yet she remained strong and full of hope. Her gentle touch seemed to make the pain more bearable. Her prayers gave new courage to the weak as they learned to lean on her and trust her. She always seemed to have time for those who needed her.

While she was home in Indiana on her second vacation, she was asked if she would be willing to go to Nepal, to do the same things all over again—help found a hospital and start a nurses' training school.

"Nepal?" she said to her sister Esther. "Who ever heard of my going to Nepal? Ha! But if God wants me to go to Nepal that's where I will go. He is as able to help me and use me there as anywhere else."

ON THE ROOF OF THE WORLD

May 28, 1957

"Dear Es,

"We had a nice smooth take-off in Patna, India, and went right along the Ganges for a short time. Then we flew over farming land and finally I could see the snow peaks in the distance. Next I saw deep jungle and finally the foothills. We flew at 10,500 feet in order to get through the pass. As we flew through it, it seemed as if the wing tips would touch the sides of the mountains, but I know they were farther away than that. Then all of a sudden we were through the pass and swooped right down into Kathmandu [Cut-mahn-doo] airport."

This was the first of Lena's letters from the mysterious land of Nepal which people on the outside sometimes called the "Closed Land," or the "Forbidden Land," or more often "The Roof of the World" because it was the home of the Himalaya Mountains. The Nepalese language reminded Lena of the Hindi spoken in India, and although she could un-

derstand it, it was different. Instead of greeting her with *Salam* they said *Namaste,* but they were equally friendly. In contrast to the heat of the plains where she had worked in India it was cool in Kathmandu, a city located at an elevation of five thousand feet. Wherever she looked she saw the towering mountains, silent and majestic, their tips covered with snow. One tip towered higher than all the rest—world famous Mount Everest. She did not know then that some of the people climbing it would come to the hospital for help.

It took the birds of Nepal to open the way for missionaries. Very few foreigners, and no missionaries, had been allowed into Nepal for hundreds of years prior to 1950. But there were many missionaries in India who were thinking of Nepal, including Dr. Robert Fleming, principal of a Christian school at Woodstock, not far from the border of Nepal. He was an ornithologist—a bird lover. He photographed birds, studied them, and mounted some for museums in North America. One year he applied to the Nepalese government for permission to study the birds of their land, and to his great joy, it was granted. It became the first of many trips during which he collected both pictures and birds for the Field Museum of Natural History in Chicago.

But Dr. Fleming did not go to Nepal alone. With him went his wife, Bethel, who was a medical doctor. And because she wanted help they had two more doctors go with them. While Dr. Robert was studying the birds, his wife Dr. Bethel and the other two doctors helped the people with treatments and medicines. Soon after their coming, the government of Nepal gave the doctors this invitation: "Would you and your people want to start a hospital for us in Nepal? Nepal is Hindu in religion and we do not want our people to become Christians, but if you can come to help us with a hospital we would be glad." How glad the missionaries were! Within three years many missionary societies had together formed the United Mission to Nepal (UMN) to bring medical help to the people. Lena Graber was invited to come to the hospital as Superintendent of Nursing and to start a nurses' training school. So here she was.

SHANTA BHAWAN HOSPITAL

"The hospital is called Shanta Bhawan, which means House of Peace," she was soon able to report. "It is made out of one of the palaces. There are three floors on the front and two sides. The back side has only two floors. . . . The senior nurses live here at the hospital on third floor, on one side overlooking the private garden, and the eternal snows on the other. Most patients make their own arrangements about food. [Relatives stay with them and cook for them.] On the first floor we have a men's ward . . . the second floor is the female ward. . . . On the third floor we have two private rooms for maternity cases. This used to be the Queen's own suite. The walls are decorated with handpainted designs of Nepalese birds and butterflies. . . .

"Our staff includes seven American nurses, one Swiss nurse, three English and three Indian nurses. Then we have three partly-trained Nepali girls, and since June 10 two Nepalese boys and two girls taking nurses' training. . . . Up to now there has been no nurses' training in Nepal.

"There is a river near here which flows through the Valley. It flows into the Ganges and is considered sacred. Not too many people die here in the hospital because when they get critically ill they are taken to the river to die. This is considered to be of much value to their souls. . . . If they do die in the hospital they are taken out through a special door at the rear, never through an entrance used for the living."

A few months after she had arrived in Nepal Lena met the King and Queen. "Thursday was the biggest day of all. We had a reception for the Executive Committee of the UMN. His Majesty, the King, and Her Majesty, the Queen, had consented to come. We arranged tours for guests to see the whole hospital. Everything really shone that day. At 3:15 the motorcycles roared up to announce the royal party's arrival. They drove up in a Dodge car. It was a real thrill when Dr. Fleming introduced me to them. For I had never even as much as seen a king or a queen before. They are really a charming couple, so simply dressed and gracious and friendly. Prince Himalaya and his wife, the second princess, were also in the party. The Prince drove his own car, also a Dodge.

"Just about fifteen minutes before the royal party arrived we had to admit a patient. And as soon as everyone had left after 5 P.M. we had to do surgery. We were glad it was not a case that had to be taken care of immediately. . . .

"Have you heard that we can buy Swiss cheese right here in Kathmandu? There are some Swiss agriculturists here who are experimenting with the making of cheese high up in the mountains. . . . It looks and tastes exactly like the kind my mother used to make when we lived in Iowa on the farm . . . . For fruit we have all the tropical kinds. Right now we are getting very sweet, juicy oranges. The radishes here are the largest I have ever seen. It is common to see them eighteen inches long and four inches in diameter."

106

Another time she wrote about the temple. "The name of this capital city is Kathmandu. The meaning of the word is 'wood temple.' They have one temple here made entirely from the wood of one tree. It has the most exquisite fine wood carving all over the outside. Inside lives what they call a living goddess. One can go and see her any day. She is a young girl about eight or ten years of age. I am not sure just how they go about choosing her. . . ."

Shanta Bhawan Hospital always came first in Lena's life. Once she was asked to take an important patient to a hospital in the United States, but she was soon back at work. "Our Shanta Bhawan Hospital," she wrote, "continues to be popular and full to the last bed and more

most of the time. I wish you could see the man who had his face lifted back into place after a bear had mauled him. I mean literally lifted for it was hanging down around his chin when he came. Or the Tibetan lady who came twenty days walk from the North after her husband had bitten or cut off her nose. Several of our doctors had a part in bringing up a tube graft to make her a new nose. She is almost ready to be discharged. Or all the many children who need to be made 'straight' because of rickets, tuberculosis, or injury. These children are often here a long time and do not want to go home when the time comes . . . Tashi is a small boy who came with such knock-knees that he had to crawl about. After his operation, even when he had lots of pain, all he could say was,

'Look! My legs are straight like yours!' It is a joy to serve them all."

SPECIAL ABILITIES

"Am I really a missionary," Lena sometimes asked herself, "or am I only a nurse away from home? I do lead devotions and prayer meetings sometimes, but I have not preached sermons, nor baptized converts for Jesus. Am I a missionary?" And at such times she often thought of her favorite Bible verse: "God has given each of you some special abilities; be sure to use them to help each other . . . ." She thought of the thousands of sick people she had helped over many years in India and now in Nepal, giving them back health and hope. She thought of how she truly loved many of them simply because Christ loved her and them both. And she knew deep in her heart that she was a missionary because she was trying to walk in the steps of Jesus, healing and helping and loving in His name.

Lena knew that it was forbidden to win people for Christ in Nepal. One woman who became a Christian had to spend six months in jail. But she knew also that the power of God was at work everywhere. One day she wrote: "The pastor who was in jail for four and one-half years was suddenly and quietly released . . . on His Majesty the King's birthday on June 11th this year. The evening of the same day there was a general meeting of all Christians here in the valley to welcome him. This surely was an answer to prayer. After recuperating for a few weeks he made a tour of all the places where there are believers and visited them all over Nepal. . . . Not long ago we welcomed a new believer into the church. So the church here continues to grow slowly."

In another letter she wrote: "This weekend is the meeting of the Nepal Christian Fellowship . . . Christians come as delegates from the Christian groups all over Nepal. Also some Gorkha soldiers who became Christians in England and who are now living in the hill villages are attending. . . . They have Bible study together, discuss problems of the new church in this country, and then each evening they have a meeting of singing, testimony, and a sermon. The evening meeting is open to non-Christians also, and it seems that quite a few are attending."

When Kanchi became a Christian she was put in jail. But she was so filled with joy and bubbling over about her faith that she was released in order not to convert the prisoners. At her trial the judge asked again and again who had made her a Christian, and she replied, "God himself did, through the reading of His Word." So the judge, Lena reported, had a Bible brought to the court and read long sections from it, even to the court. Then he said, "These words will not harm our people." Kanchi could go free.

It was, Lena thought, as Dr. Robert Fleming often said: "If Christianity is any good, it will speak for itself to these people."

As she worked with the student nurses she knew she was being watched by them. "Therefore," she wrote, "we are constantly faced with the importance of walking before them as we ought. Keep praying for these girls and others throughout Nepal who want to follow Christ. The law of the land still does not allow them to openly be His disciples."

LIFEBUOY SOAP AND WARM WATER

As more workers became available the hospital staff sent teams of nurses into the villages to help people with their diseases and to teach simple health rules.

One time when the nurse in charge was ill Lena volunteered to do this. She took along two students every day to help her and, more importantly, to teach them how to do it. "We have gone all over the valley," she wrote, "as far as we could walk in one day. . . . When we find someone who needs help, we stop and help them. Usually it is sores on their hands or feet. While one of the students takes care of these I give the health lesson to the people. Then we go on again . . . .

"We found a twelve-day-old baby covered with Pemphigus. . . . As soon as it began getting the blisters the mother stopped bathing it, thinking this was the thing to do. So the girls bathed it well with Lifebuoy soap and warm water in the sunshine. After it was dried we painted it with Mercurochrome and then put some antibiotic ointment on it. We told the mother to get some soap and wash it like we did every day. 'As clean as a cat' is our slogan. . . . In a few days we went back and found it much better . . . .

"In the same village an old man came with a big sore on the top of his foot. A cow had stepped on it. I do not know what he had put on the sore because he would not tell us. I presume it was cow's urine, for this is the common treatment for sores in the villages. This is why soap and water and Mercurochrome do so much good. Even if it isn't considered terribly effective in the USA, it is a good deal better than the village treatment of cow's urine . . . .

"In another home we went to check up on a former patient in our hospital. The baby was about a year old. When we got there we found only the children at home. . . . We found the year-old-baby and the twin brother, and another brother four years old, and two sisters aged eight and nine. They had hardly any clothes on . . . . We left some food for the baby. . . .

The next time we went out to the village we took some clothes along for each of the children. The mother again was not home because she works all day in Patan. We took each of the little ones and gave them a soap and water bath and put them into clean clothes . . . . The women and other children of the village came to watch us work. I gave a lesson on worms and cleanliness in general. When we left, one of the students said, 'When the mother comes home in the evening she will think she is having a dream.' "

Is My Work Done?

The years sped by. Each day was filled from early till late with service for others. The Shanta Bhawan Hospital expanded and was modernized. More workers came. Many Nepalese workers had graduated from the Nursing School and were reaching into every corner of Nepal with their love and care. Gradually Lena began to ask herself, "Is my work done here now? Do they still need me?" The day came when she decided to return home to Indiana and the house she would live in with her sister Esther. The hospital sadly agreed to let her go, and sent the following letter to her mission board:

"Whereas Miss Graber . . . Nursing School Superintendent at SBH, is requesting to withdraw her service with the UMN at the close of her present term of service in September 1967, it was RESOLVED to express sincere gratitude for years of faithful service in the Mission and to welcome her return to service again if she should so desire . . . ."

When Lena read these words she said, "I have only done what any Christian would do for Jesus and His children in need."

It was hard for Lena to leave the hospital and all the friends and workers after so many years, but they told her,

108

"Who knows, Lena, you may be back before you know it."

That is exactly what happened. A few years later an emergency developed in the hospital and the call came to Lena—could she come back to help them for a year? Of course she went. Had not the Apostle Peter long ago said, "God has given each of you some special abilities; be sure to use them to help each other . . . "?

What else could you do if you wanted to follow Jesus?

10

Joe Walks Along

I have been asked to tell you the story of my life. I am glad to do it. It will be an Indian story because I am an Indian American. The history books you use in school say very little about Indians or about America when it belonged to them, and what they say is often wrong. The Indians you see on television do not help you to know us either. Perhaps my story will help you understand my people.

I am an American of the Cheyenne nation, which calls itself *Wohehiv,* and means "The Morning Star People." Many years ago we called ourselves the *Tse-Tses-Tasso* nation, which means "The Real People." When our fathers later came in contact with the Sioux tribe they called us *Sha-hi-ena,* meaning "Those Who Talk Red," because they could not understand us. When the white man came he spoke this name like it sounded to him—Cheyenne. But our people want to be known as "The Morning Star People." The morning star has always been important to us. It gives us fresh courage every morning, for it tells us the dawn will soon come.

We are not really Indians like everybody calls us. The name "Indian" was given to us by mistake. When Columbus landed on our shores he was lost. He thought he had discovered India, and so we were called Indians. By the time people found out that America was not India, it was too late to change the name.

But Indians prefer to be called by the name of their nation or tribe, or simply Americans or Canadians.

I was born on the Cheyenne reservation in southeastern Montana. A reservation is land which the government has reserved for Indians only. Unfortunately, it is often the poorest land of all, left after the white man has taken what he wanted. There are seven reservations in Montana. The Cheyenne reservation is small but the land is good for grazing cattle.

My father's name was *Nanoseham,* which means "Mountain Lion." He was an honored man among the Cheyenne people. When he grew old he asked me to take his place in the Council, but I gave him no answer. I was not ready for that responsibility. My grandfather was Yellow Robe. He fought in the battle at the Little Horn River in 1876, in which General Custer and his men were killed.

When I was born, the government recorder demanded an English name. He wrote down "Walks Along" because that was the name of my grandmother. Then he asked, "And what's his first name?"

But he did not understand Cheyenne, and so he said, "We'll call him Joseph—Joe," and wrote it down.

Cheyenne families do not use family names in their language. Each member of the family had his own name until government regulations made us take English family names. A man might give his name to someone he wished to honor in a special way. When that happened, he took a new name for himself and never used the old one again.

MY FATHERS WERE GREAT MEN

When I started school in Lame Deer I could not speak English. A boy next to me interpreted for me. He wrote my name "Joe" on a piece of paper and told me to copy it. We had a white teacher. She did not have time for me. She was impatient with me, and I felt she did not like me. This made me feel lonely. She did not know our Indian life and history. Soon I began running away from school right after lunch when all the children were playing. It was much more fun to walk across the hills and feel the wind in my hair. Sometimes I hunted rabbits or fished in the stream. When evening came I would go home happy and free.

Our family was poor. My father had a few cattle, but there were no jobs on the reservation or in Lame Deer. My mother used to go down the back alleys in town to find scraps of meat in the garbage. I loved my parents, especially my father. He was never angry with me. If I had done something wrong, my uncles would come and punish me, as was our Indian custom. They threatened to drown me in the river. I was very afraid of them, but not of my father. He was my best friend.

I will never forget the stories my father told me about life among the Cheyenne nation long ago. Many, many ages ago our people used to live in the woodland country around the Great Lakes. Then they began moving westward until they came to the Red River in what is now Minnesota and the Dakotas. They did some hunting, but game was scarce. Most of their food came from gardens. Their houses, made of earth, were partly underground.

There had never been horses in America until the Spaniards brought them along from Europe. Some of these ran away and multiplied on the prairies until large troops of wild and free mustangs galloped across the plains. Our fathers found that they could ride them, and that changed everything. Now they could hunt for food many miles away from home. They could run down and kill all the buffalo they wanted. The buffalo skins made good tepees which were cool in summer and warm in winter and could be moved easily. Soon the earth houses were forgotten, and my fathers moved wherever there was good hunting and fresh water.

This moving around took them to the lands of other Indian tribes and brought trouble over hunting rights. The horse was good for war. A band of warriors could swoop down on a tepee village and be gone again in a minute. The fighting braves could hide from the arrows of their enemies by hanging low on the side of the horses. Soon a good horse was the prize possession of every Indian man.

White Americans often think of Indians as having been cruel and bloodthirsty. That is not true. The Cheyennes were a particularly peaceful nation, but they were not cowards. When the white man took more and more of their land and destroyed village after village, the Indians finally fought back in order to survive. White men did not know one tribe from another. "The only good Indian is a dead one," they used to say.

One day Cheyenne hunters found twenty steers which had wandered away from the white settlers' herd and chased them many miles back to their owners. But the owners said the Indians had stolen them, and called soldiers to hunt them down. The soldiers came upon Chief Lean Bear with a party of braves on the hunt. He had been in Washington the year before and met President Lincoln, who had given him a medal. Chief Lean Bear held up his medal and identification papers and rode out to meet them, but the soldiers opened fire and killed him, together with twenty-six of his men.

That same year the territorial governor of Colorado called on all citizens to "kill and destroy" the Indians. When our fathers heard this they sent a friend to Colonel Chivington, the commander of the area, to assure him of our desire for peace.

But the Colonel, who incidentally had once been a minister, said, "Scalps are what we are after; kill and scalp all Indians—big ones and little ones."

A short time later his troops stormed over the village and killed over three hundred of our people. Two women, five children, and Chief Black Kettle escaped. All the rest perished. But they had done no wrong. After that our people planned revenge. They called the Colonel "Squaw Killer."

No one hated us more than did Colonel George A. Custer, who made a name for himself killing Indians. Early on the morning of November 27, 1868, for example, he and his men quietly surrounded a Cheyenne village near the Washita River and then attacked. Chief Black Kettle and 103 of his people perished. The whites then found out that it had been a friendly Cheyenne village, but Custer said the massacre was "a great and gallant victory for our beloved country."

Revenge came eight years later, on June 25, 1876, when Custer rode into a trap he had planned for our people. He

and every one of his soldiers were killed, 265 in all. But many Indian braves also perished. The battlefield is now a tourist attraction forty miles west of my home in Lame Deer.

Soon more white troops arrived, and the Northern Cheyenne were herded south to Oklahoma where the Southern Cheyenne lived. It was hot and humid there. My fathers were used to the mountains. Many died from disease and starvation. Finally they decided to fight their way back to Montana. The army tried to stop them, but about three hundred escaped under the leadership of chief Morning Star and Chief Little Wolf. It was a bitter trek during cold winter months, with little food, and soldiers always hunting for them. But they made it back. Then the government in Washington ordered them returned to Oklahoma. They refused and were put into log prisons that had no plaster left in the cracks. They had no heat, no blankets, and no food. To stay alive they ate the bark off the logs in the wall and even their moccasins. Finally they could stand it no longer and broke out the night of January 9, 1879, only to be shot down by the soldiers. Many hid in the snow, but sixty-four were killed. The government allowed those who remained alive to stay in Montana, but put them on a small reservation. The white man owned most of the land by that time.

These are the stories my father and my uncles and the wise men of our Cheyenne nation told us when I was young. I have not forgotten them. Today I tell them to my own children.

I JOINED THE ARMY

When I was in grade school I was very shy. Sometimes I walked home along the creek instead of on the road in order not to meet people. I did not mind studying, but what good would it do me? I was only an Indian and had no future in American society. No Indian even taught in our own schools at that time. I had only white teachers. But I started high school anyway. I rode a bus to Colstrip, twenty-three miles away.

One day when I came home from school my mother said, "Joe, there is a letter for you."

Never before had anyone written to me. I suspected that it would be a draft call from the government to order me to fight for my country. It was. "What else is there for me to do anyway?" I thought. So I joined the army.

A leader of the Peyote religion arranged for a farewell ceremony and gave me a little cactus plant in a pouch. "Wear this around your neck," he said. "Never take it off. It is a good luck charm and will bring you back safely to us."

The army wanted to make tough fighters out of us quickly and drilled us hard. I had good food and clothing. I didn't have to make decisions or plan my life; I only had to obey orders. After a time the order came for my unit to go to Korea to fight the Communists. Over there the trucks hauled us to the front lines where the shooting was going on. We were afraid, but went anyway. It is hard to see your friends shot, so we tried to get the enemy first. Once when the fighting and dying got very bad the chaplain came and prayed with us. "Trust God and be a good soldier," he said. "You will soon be sent back home to rest."

I was often depressed and lonely, especially if no mail came from home. Missionary Alfred Habegger, who knew me from the reservation, did write to me. In 1954, after two years in Korea, I came back to Montana.

LIQUOR

There was nothing for me to do when I returned to the reservation. There was no liquor on the reservation, but there was at the Jimtown Bar four miles away. Since I had learned to drink in the army, I began spending more and more time at the bar. Still I didn't want to.

One day I decided to turn over a new leaf. I would go into business for myself. To do this I needed money. The Veterans' Administration had money to lend to returning soldiers for this purpose. I filled out application forms and waited, while my plans for a cattle ranch of my own grew more exciting every day. But when I went to find out the answer I was told, "We are sorry, Mr. Walks Along, your application has been turned down."

"Why?" I asked bewildered.

"Your credit is not strong enough," they said.

They meant I was a poor risk and would probably fail. I went to the bar and got very drunk.

Soon I was in trouble with the police for being drunk and for getting liquor for minors. The first time they locked me up I managed to crawl up the wall to a window at the top and was about to escape when they found me. I was put into solitary confinement for ninety days. It was a small room six by four feet without a window, except a little one in the door so the guards could watch me. They gave me one magazine a week to read, nothing else, not even a radio. I was lonely and depressed. Life seemed meaningless.

Not long after I was out, a friend and I were caught again for the same offense. As the policeman brought us into the office of the Justice of the Peace he said, "I think we got the two worst drunks on the reservation right here."

We had to sit and wait for about three hours until the JP had finished his dice game. Then he locked us up again for ninety days.

I knew I was as rough and tough as a man could be and it troubled me. I remembered that when I was a kid, I thought I could make something of myself if I could only find a way. I had told myself then that I was never going to touch alcohol. And now I was a drunk Indian. Even my own people had no use for me. People are afraid of an Indian when he's drunk. I could see the mess my personal life was in. People couldn't put their trust or confidence in me, no matter what I tried to do.

I became sick in the jail. My friend was in solitary across the hall. He knew some gospel songs. One day he found "The Old Rugged Cross" in a copy of *Life* magazine which he had been given, and he sang it to cheer me up.

The song awakened in me a deep longing for a happier life. Surely, I thought, there must be more to life than jail and liquor.

GOD

Then I learned to know two people who loved me and trusted me. I began to feel ashamed of myself and wanted to change for their sake. The first was Victoria, whom I came to love very much. Her real name was Haseoveae. I realized that she loved me, too, except when I was drinking. The other person was Alfred Habegger, the Mennonite missionary pastor on the reservation.

Long before this time a young Christian from Switzerland had come to the Cheyenne nation as a missionary. His name was Rodolfe Petter. He was the first to put our language into writing. Then he wrote a grammar for it. He translated the whole New Testament and latter half of the Old Testament into Cheyenne. Now our people could read about Jesus and study God's Word for themselves. I noticed that many lives were being changed. My father and mother became Christians.

Alfred Habegger cared for me. When I came walking down the street he often came out to the mailbox and waited to talk to me. My friends would say, "Why do you let him bother you? Just punch him in the nose." But I never did.

I was not afraid of a preacher, and I noticed that he was not afraid of me either. He was really interested in me. Once he said, "You know, Joe, those beer cans don't look too good by the side of your house, do they?"

But he never scolded me or talked down to me. He never forced the love of Jesus down my throat. He just loved me in the name of Jesus. My lonely heart began to respond. I had been searching for something better for a long time. I began to feel that I was finding it.

Victoria noticed the change, too, and one day we were married. Soon after that we came to church regularly and began to help in its work.

One day Alfred Habegger said, "Joe and Victoria, would you like to go to Bible school?"

We looked at each other, speechless. But he continued, "The Cook Christian Training School in Phoenix, Arizona, has a four-year Bible study program for young people. Will you think and pray about whether God might be calling you to go there?"

We said, "Yes," but when we talked about it, we doubted.

I had not finished all of my senior year in high school. Besides, where would we get the money? Yet something within us kept saying, "Go."

We know it was God's Spirit leading

us. I finished high school in two months, and the government agreed to finance my studies under their veterans' education program. Soon we were on our way to Phoenix, anxious but very thankful.

I worked hard in school. It was such a joy to study the Bible day after day. I felt a deep hunger to know more of God's will for mankind and for me. I never missed school, and my grades were good. In the last year I was chosen student body president. I also worked hard after school to earn extra money to buy groceries and clothing. Victoria had her hands more than full with our three oldest boys—James, Joseph, Jr., and Billy. I worked at a chicken farm and any odd jobs I could find.

One day the police stopped me as I was going to the rich part of town to paint a house I had agreed to do.

"What are you doing here?" they asked suspiciously. I told them and they finally let me go.

Another time the police treated me roughly when I had a flat tire on the school van. They were convinced I had stolen it. They didn't trust me at all. But it didn't bother me anymore. I had inner joy and self-respect and could remain calm with them. God had worked a change in my life. A verse from the Apostle Paul's letter to the Ephesians had helped me a great deal: "So then you are no longer strangers and sojourners, but you are fellow citizens with the saints and members of the household of God" (2:19). I no longer felt lonely or unwanted. I was a member of the family of God himself. If other people thought I was "just another Indian," that was their problem.

BACK TO LAME DEER

While still at school before graduation, the Petter Memorial Church, as our Cheyenne church was called, asked me to be their pastor. This was a terribly difficult decision for me to make. The church calls for clean people—special people—to be its leaders. I didn't feel that I qualified because of my past. But I knew too that Jesus had forgiven me and I was clean.

The criticism I received from old drinking friends was another part of my struggle in deciding whether to become a minister. But others told me to forget what these were saying. They told me the call to the ministry was the important thing. It was encouraging to me to realize that my calling was to stand before these very people who criticized me and give them God's message. In 1960 I accepted the call for a one-year trial period. I am still serving there.

When I first started to preach, my old drinking friends came to church and laughed at me; but I kept on and they finally stopped. I found great strength in Psalm 27:1: "The Lord is my light and my salvation; whom shall I fear? The Lord is the stronghold of my life; of whom shall I be afraid?"

I told all of them that Christ is the salvation from eternal destruction as well as the answer to life's needs here, not just in the hereafter. The eternal starts now. "I give you this life," Christ said, "if you believe in me." This is how I explain it to the Cheyenne.

It is still difficult for people to believe that Christ is alive and at work in us. But I tell them that He will help them in every area of daily life, at work, in the home, in conversation with people, and in the way they conduct themselves. Teenagers sometimes think religion is don't, don't, don't. It's not that. When you really love Christ, it's a wonderful life. You see life altogether differently.

Life on the reservation is a battle for the Cheyennes. It is for every Indian American. There are few jobs, poor land, no future. Many of our young people drift to the cities, but they are lonely there, and people take advantage of them because they are not white. There are a few factories in our area now, but women work beside men in them all day. We are not used to that in our culture and it brings problems.

Many of our people become so discouraged that they commit suicide, especially young people. The highest suicide rate in the United States is among the Northern Cheyennes. Not long ago I heard a group of white Mennonite young people sing at a conference. They sang beautifully. I said to myself, "Why can't my Cheyenne young people sing like that?"

Not long ago a young woman came to me for help. I tried to help. She went away, left her baby with a friendly family, and killed herself. Then I felt I had failed my Lord and my people. Why couldn't I help her? What are our young people looking for, I asked myself. I know that they can only be helped through Jesus Christ working in people who love them. We are now trying to raise money for a youth center building.

It is difficult to help when society does not care. White Americans are proud to have a little Indian blood in them, but not too much. Did you know that Indians were not granted citizenship by Congress until 1924, 317 years after the first white settlers came to our shores? And even so, why should Congress give us citizenship when we have always been Americans?

I am glad that there is peace between us and the white man now. I very much like a poem written by Alexander Posey, a Cree Indian.

Pledge of Peace

I pledge you by the moon and sun,
As long as stars their course shall
*   run,*
Long as day shall meet my view,
Peace shall reign between us two.

I pledge you by those peaks of
*   snow,*
As long as streams to ocean flow,
Long as years their youth renew,
Peace shall reign between us two.

I came from mother soil and cave;
You came from pathless sea and
*   wave;*
Strangers fought our battles thru:
Peace shall reign between us two.

I too want peace. But can there really be true peace until we have found our way back to dignity and self-respect as Indian people? The white man has taken our land, our future, and nearly destroyed us as a people. These old wrongs can be made right only by doing right now. When election time draws near, every politician talks about helping the Indian, but nothing much happens afterwards. Dozens of scholars come and study us. I think they know more about us than God does, but nothing much changes here. Their students, of course, get another new book to read.

My hope remains in Christ and in His people, the Church. We have formed the Mennonite Indian Leaders Council (MILC) in North America to work together on common problems. But we have a long way to go. Even well-meaning Christians do not always understand us. A white church brother and I were standing by a river. Suddenly he said, "Joe, if you were still an Indian, could you shoot an arrow across the water to the other side?"

But this is also my ministry—to help people see I do not need to be white to be a Christian. Perhaps the boys and girls who read my story will help us to change things faster. We have a Tourist Center and Campground at Lame Deer, and would enjoy visiting with them. If they wish, they can even rent a tepee to sleep in for the night.

11

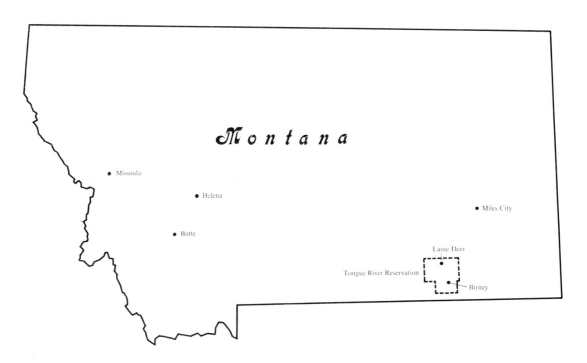

Suhadiweko Djojodihardjo
(Pak Djojo)

God loved the world so much that he gave his only Son, that everyone who has faith in him may not die but have eternal life. JOHN 3:16

Would you like to visit a beautiful island far away in the Indian Ocean? And live there long enough to enjoy the warm sunshine, high mountains, beautiful birds, and banana trees? Then come with me to our home in the Muria Mountains of Java. Be my guest until we know each other. Let me tell you a story, my story—and then you can return to your own land again.

My name is a long one as you can see. Try pronouncing it like this — Soo-ha-dee-vay-ko Jo-yo-di-har-jo. It is too long to use often, but it has a beautiful meaning. My parents put the way they felt when I was born, and their hopes for me, into my name. Suhadiweko means— more, precious, and careful; Djojo-dihardjo means success and blessed. Most people just call me Pa' Joyo. Pak is a form of address used for all grown men in our country and means father. Call me Pa' Joyo.

I live in Indonesia, which is a part of Asia. Our country consists of three thousand islands spread across three thousand miles of ocean. One of these islands is very small, but is known to many tourists for its beautiful climate and sandy beaches. It is the island of Bali. The island of Java, where I live, is much larger. Its population is eighty million, more than that of any of the other islands, and half of all the people in Indonesia. People live closer together in Java than anywhere else in the world. I live in the north-central part of the island, in the town of Pati, near the city of Semarang.

Most of the people of Indonesia are Moslems who belong to the religion of Islam, but a few are Buddhists or Hindus. Only two persons out of every one hundred are Christians. I am a fourth generation Christian because my great-grandfather became a believer in Jesus Christ 150 years ago.

Do you know any missionaries who have worked in Asia? We often had missionaries in our home when I was a little boy. Soon I wanted to be a missionary too, which I thought meant learning how to preach. My poor mother and sisters and my only brother often had to listen to me preach at that time. I am sure they did not enjoy it very much. As a little boy I knew the church and already loved Jesus.

The first Mennonite missionaries to come to Java were Pieter Jansz and his new bride who were sent from Holland in 1851. Pieter taught school near Dje-pora in the Muria Mountain region. He used every possible opportunity to tell people about Jesus Christ. After three years he baptized five persons and had the Lord's Supper together with them. It was a slow beginning. "People who believe do not hurry," he used to say. After he knew the language well enough he translated the entire Bible into Javanese.

One day he decided to buy a large

piece of land and establish a Christian colony on it. He wanted to have a place where people would help each other and where they would not be tempted by their old friends and habits. Later some missionaries came from the Mennonite communities in Russia to help him. The colony did not work too well, however, until his son Pieter, who also became a missionary, worked with it many years later. The missionaries from Russia continued to help there, too.

I was born in one of these Christian villages called Margoredjo. My father was a teacher and preacher in the village. I remember that he prayed a great deal. He had long prayers during family devotions; at least they seemed long to me. Sometimes at night, when I woke up, I would see him kneeling beside his bed and hear the low murmur of his voice as he prayed. He told us that he was often afraid of all the problems he faced in teaching and church work. He was also concerned about earning enough money for bread for his large family. But his fears went away and he received courage when he prayed. I pray much today, too. I think my father taught me this, and I am very grateful to him for it.

School Can Be Fun

When I was six years old I was enrolled in our village school. I enjoyed it very much because I knew nearly everyone and because the teacher was a Christian. Four lears later I graduated and had to go to Kudus which was some distance away. My mother thought I had studied enough now and should stay home. But my father said, "He is only ten years old. He cannot get a job like a man. I think he should go to school." So my mother let me go.

She said no more about my staying home after I had finished the school in Kudus four years later, so I went on to high school in Semarang, the capital city of the province.

Now I had an important decision to make. Should I go on to a seminary and become a missionary or minister as I had always wanted, or should I study medicine and become a doctor? I wanted to do both, but did not see how I could. I prayed about it. I asked my friends what they thought I should do. One day I met a missionary whom I knew. I asked him what he thought I should do.

"Why," he replied, "I think the answer is clear. There is such a shortage of doctors in Java that I think you should by all means become a doctor, a *Christian* doctor."

But later I talked again with my father, and he said, "Djojo, what Java needs most is the gospel. Let others study medicine. Come and help us make Christ known to our people."

Deep in my heart I knew he was right. So I went to seminary far away in Djakarta.

School had always been fun for me, but now I did not enjoy it anymore. I was a grown man, but that was not the reason. I was far from home, but that was not the reason either. I felt I was losing my faith in God. My teachers told me so much about the Bible that I began to believe it was not true, and that my father had been kind but wrong in his preaching and praying. The more I studied the Bible the less I knew for sure.

Finally I said to myself, "Tomorrow I am leaving school for good. The Bible is just not true like my father said it was. I don't even know whether I believe in God anymore. I might as well be honest and admit it."

It was early morning when I got up from my study desk and went to bed. But I could not sleep. So I got up again and sat in the big, soft chair next to my bed. My heart cried out, "Lord, if You do exist, speak to me. This is the last time I am coming to You."

As I sat there with my eyes closed I suddenly saw a vision. I was floating through the air ever so gently, and I heard a voice coming from the glittering sky around me, saying, "I know what you want to know."

I asked, "Who are you? What do you know about me?"

The voice replied, "I know what you want to know. Listen. It is this, only this: God loved the world—and you, Djojo—so much that He gave His only Son, that everyone—including you, Djojo —who has faith in Him may not die, but have eternal life."

I heard myself responding, "Yes, that is what I want to know."

Then I realized I was still sitting in the same soft chair by my bed. But I was changed. I felt so free. My fear was gone. I felt only joy and peace.

I said aloud to myself, "Now you teachers can say what you wish about the Bible. I know what I know, and no one can take it away from me."

Now studying was enjoyable again, more enjoyable than ever before. I felt God was very close and I was studying to understand Him and to serve Him.

WAR, WAR

I had just finished seminary when the Japanese armies invaded Indonesia in 1941. They drove out the Dutch who had ruled our country for 350 years. There was terrible fighting. Soldiers and guns and dead people were everywhere. The train on which I was returning home from school was bombed. I escaped unharmed, but the boxes with all my books were destroyed. I had saved and worked for six years to buy them. Now they were gone. But I had been carrying my Bible when the train was hit and so I had it, fortunately.

We had a particularly difficult time in our own community in the Muria Mountains. The Dutch armies had gone, but the Japanese armies had not yet arrived. This gave the Moslems an opportunity to destroy the work of the Christians, whom they hated. At first a small group formed, but soon there were over one thousand Moslems marching and shouting Sabil, Sabil, which meant "holy war." They were bent on destroying churches, hospitals, and other Christian work. They came to Tayu, where they beat and tortured the hospital staff and left Dr. Ong lying half-dead on the street. Then they went on. Before they came to my home village of Margoredjo they sent word that every Christian must renounce his faith in Christ or be killed. On the way they destroyed a church and beat the Christians they could find. Many Christians fled to the forests to find protection from the mob. When the mob arrived in Margoredjo they mistreated many Christians and completely destroyed the church. Some Christians gave up their faith because they feared suffering and possible death.

At that time my father was the preacher in Pati, a larger town. One day the crowds became angry with the Christians, and the Christians met together in the church. As my father prayed in his house behind the church, the people in the church saw a vision of a white-robed man with his arms stretched heavenward. They gained strength from the vision, and the angry crowd did no harm.

Soon after this I married Armini, whom I had known as a student. We were asked to serve the church in Margoredjo. I was watched very closely by the Japanese army and police. They thought I might stir the people up against them. I often hid in the hills, fields, and barns during the daytime, coming home at night for food. I prayed much when I was hiding and I read the Bible. By the time it was safe for me to live at home again I had read the New Testament four times and the Old Testament twice.

One night we had a church council meeting in our house. Suddenly we were interrupted by a knock on the door. The house was surrounded by the police. They arrested me and took me to the police station.

"What were you doing in that house?" they asked. "Were you planning a revolution?"

"Only against the devil," I replied. They laughed and finally let me go.

People often came to ask me to help them and to pray for them. One day I was called to a house where a man lived with his wife and mother-in-law. The wife was very sick, and the man blamed the mother-in-law for the sickness. So he beat her. When I saw what had happened I became very angry and asked him how he could expect his wife to get well if he beat his mother-in-law. I said God would surely judge him unless he repented from his sin. When the man was sorry for his evil deed, I laid my hands on his sick wife to pray for her recovery.

When I was finished she said, "Something happened to me just now. I feel much better. I think I will live."

Soon many people came to me for prayer because they had heard I could heal them. Some thought I was a *Dukun*, which means a witch doctor, but I told them about Christ and the power of faith in Him.

Finally the war with the Japanese came to an end, but then our national revolution began. Our country was trying to free itself from the Dutch colonial government. Sometimes our area was controlled by the Dutch army, sometimes by the Indonesian army. The Dutch officials did not trust the Christians because they suspected us of being revolutionaries. The Indonesian officials did not trust the Christians because they thought that if we believed in the Dutch religion we would also help the Dutch army. So it was very hard for us. Many bands of robbers and guerrillas roamed through the countryside and there was very little food anywhere.

We had three children by now and I could not find enough food for them. One day Armini came and said, "Djojo, there is no food. I have been unable to find any in the village or on the fields, and we have no money. What shall we do?"

It was four o'clock in the afternoon. I went to the church and kneeled to pray.

I said, "Dear God, you have helped us so often. We belong to you. Help us now, I pray, that my family may have food. You know I have nothing left to sell. Help us. Amen."

I prayed for about an hour. Armini met me at the door when I came back. She was crying.

"Look, Djojo," she said, "someone brought us some food. We can eat. But why do we have to ask God for it? He knows we need it without our asking."

"Armini," I answered, "God loves us. He is testing and strengthening our faith. Now let us sit down and eat. I am hungry."

For some time the Dutch army was in control of our area, and the police watched me closely because they thought I was a revolutionary. One day the chief officer of our residency threatened to jail me, and I replied, "I am a Christian, not a political revolutionary. I follow Jesus and no one else. You may jail me, of course, but that will not stop the work of God. One day there will be a strong church in Indonesia."

So he told his men, "Do not jail him, but watch him."

Some weeks later when we were again without food and praying to God for help, the policeman who was assigned to watch me came with a package of food and said, "I don't know why I am doing this, but something tells me to bring it here."

Then he left.

"Look," I said to Armini and the children, "God can use anyone to do His will, even those who are against Him."

How often we prayed, "Give us this day our daily bread," and in some way or other God always helped.

A New Beginning

In 1949 my father became very ill. He called me to his home and said, "I am going to be with Jesus soon. I am so glad you are serving Him. Carry on. Do not be afraid."

I had deep peace when he died, because I knew he had gone *home*.

Soon after that I was elected to be chairman of our church conference. The church seemed to be dying. The war and suffering had scattered the members so that where there had been over five thousand before the war, there were now only two thousand, including children, left. There seemed to be no courage to carry on.

The Reformed Church, a large and strong conference, sent men to us who said, "You are too small to carry on alone. Why don't you join us?" But this would mean the end of the church of our fathers and its witness to faith, love, and believers' baptism. Should we do that? We agreed to call a conference of all our people to decide what should be done.

We met for three days at the conference, often talking until late at night. When we became tired or drowsy the women brought us coffee. We were also encouraged by the presence of Daniel Amstutz, a former missionary who had been forced to leave because of the war and who had returned just in time for the conference. We talked and prayed. As chairman, I told the assembly how God had led in our church for many years. He had helped each one of us. The people interrupted me again and again, saying, "We want to talk about what you just said," or "Stop, we want to pray now." And in the end we knew God was calling us to grow in faith and hope. We knew He had work for us to do in Indonesia.

Not long after this the Mennonite Central Committee sent Orie O. Miller to visit us. God himself had sent him. He told us of our brothers and sisters around the world who loved us. He asked us what our biggest needs were, and we knew they were food and clothing. We also asked for help to begin a training school for church workers. Our friends in Holland, Germany, Switzerland, and France also sent help, and a year later we had a small school. Soon workers were going from it into many communities, teaching and preaching the good news of Jesus Christ. Young men also came from North America under MCC to help with the school and with agriculture.

Our Chinese Brothers

I have told you about the missionaries from Holland and Russia who worked with our people long ago, but I have not told you about our brothers living right here in the Muria Mountains of Java. They are the Chinese Mennonites who have been here for many years. They became Mennonite Christians without any missionary help. It is an interesting story.

Long ago a man named Tee Siem Tat, who was a Chinese-Indonesian businessman here, became very ill. He sent for a doctor who examined him and said, "Pak Tee, there is nothing wrong with you."

"But I am sick," Pak Tee replied, "I feel terrible."

"I'm sorry," the doctor responded, "perhaps you should call another doctor who may be able to help you."

He did. First one, and then another, and another. All of them said, "Pak Tee, I find nothing wrong with you."

Meanwhile Pak Tee's wife had found a Bible somewhere and had begun reading it. Every time she came to Mark 15, or other passages which told of Jesus dying on the cross, she began to cry. Finally she and Pak Tee decided to visit the Salvation Army center at Rembang to find out more about the Bible and the Christian life. Pak Tee noticed that he felt much better after the service. Soon he was completely well. They invited the Salvation Army to hold services in their own home, and one day he was converted.

Pak Tee was a very energetic man. He wanted to find out what other Christians believed and so he visited many churches and missionaries. In time, he came to believe that the teaching of missionary Johann Thiessen from Russia was closest to what he thought the Bible said, and he decided to become a Mennonite. Missionary Thiessen baptized him on December 6, 1920, along with twenty-five others whom he had already won to Christ.

Often the new Christians he won did not know what to do with their old idols. They did not have the courage to destroy their former gods on whom they had counted for so long and to whom they had prayed. So Pak Tee would offer to take them along home and store them, which he did. By the time he died in 1940, there were several hundred Christians in the church and many idols in Pak Tee's shed. After his death the family burned the idols so they would not be a temptation to anyone to forsake Christ and return to paganism.

The church kept on growing because the members themselves did the witnessing to others. Today the Chinese Mennonite church has over two thousand members. They are our brothers and sisters in Christ. We work together.

JOY AND PEACE

Our churches, too, have been growing since that conference day when we were only two thousand, including children. Today we have over twenty thousand members and with the children, over thirty thousand. Last year one of our pastors, a woman, baptized over three hundred persons herself. Many villages are asking us to send evangelists to them to teach about Jesus in their schools and churches.

People often ask about the secret of the new strength and joy in our churches. In 1967 when I went to the Mennonite World Conference in Holland, I was asked to tell about it there, and in 1969 also in Africa, and even in Manitoba, Canada. We have no secret; it is simply God at work in the power of the Holy Spirit. I have turned my life over to Him to do with me as He pleases, as have many others in our churches.

Before I let the Holy Spirit run my life I was often anxious and worried because I felt *I* had to do it. I know people say that I am a cheerful and happy person by nature, but I often did not feel that way at all. I also became angry very easily. I felt as if I had to run the whole world by myself, at least the Mennonite world in Indonesia. But after letting God guide my life by His Spirit I felt a deep joy and peace. I do not get angry like I used to because Christ lives in me. My life is now filled with thankfulness and praise to God. Deep in my innermost being I always have a feeling of joy. When people come to me for help I can now understand them more quickly and truly.

Sometimes God is still pleased to heal people through me. A woman member of our church was sick with cancer. The doctor said it had spread to all parts of her body and he could not help her. She would die soon. One day three ministers from our church and I went to see her and to pray with her. While I was praying, one of the ministers in a vision saw the cancer tumor disappear. When the woman felt her stomach she said, "It is gone. It is gone." She went to the doctor again and he said that she was healed, but he did not know how it could have happened. At another time God used my prayers to drive an evil

spirit out of two teen-age girls, and later out of a young man. This is what was promised to us by God long ago when the church began, as we read in Acts 1:8: "But you will receive power when the Holy Spirit comes upon you; and you will bear witness for me in Jerusalem, and all over Judaea and Samaria, and away to the ends of the earth."

We are a happy family. I wish you could come and visit us some time. We might be a little crowded in our house, but we could find room. Our son is studying medicine now, and one of our daughters is a lawyer, but five of our daughters are still at home. My sister and her eight children also live with us, as well as needy students and others. We have been twenty-eight persons in our house for a time. We have enough to eat, but often there are more outstanding bills than there is money. But we know from long experience that God will not forget us. At the right time His help will come. It always does.

12